# Calvin and Bullinger
# on the
# Lord's Supper

## by Paul Rorem

*Associate Professor of Ancient Church History, Lutheran School of Theology, Chicago, U.S.A.*

## THE ALCUIN CLUB and the GROUP FOR RENEWAL OF WORSHIP (GROW)

The Alcuin Club, which exists to promote the study of Christian liturgy in general and of Anglican liturgy in particular, traditionally published a single volume annually for its members. This ceased in 1986. Similarly, GROW was responsible from 1975 to 1986 for the quarterly 'Grove Liturgical Studies'. Since the beginning of 1987 the two have sponsored a Joint Editorial Board to produce quarterly 'Joint Liturgical Studies'.

## THE COVER PICTURE

reproduces the original Latin title of the *Consensus Tigurinus*

*First Impression* December 1989
**ISSN** 0951-2667
**ISBN** 1 85174 133 X

**GROVE BOOKS LIMITED**
Bramcote    Nottingham    NG9 3DS

# CONTENTS

## ACKNOWLEDGMENTS

The author and publishers express their gratitude to *The Lutheran Quarterly* for permission to reprint the two major articles first published in that journal in 1988 in Vol. 2, nos. 2 and 3, and here bound together for the first time.

# Part I. The Impasse

An investigation of the sixteenth-century Reformed views of the Lord's Supper requires much more than a detailed presentation of John Calvin's sacramental theology. Apart from the independent contributions of other Reformed theologians, Calvin's own views of the Lord's Supper were clarified and developed through dialogue, especially with his fellow Swiss pastors and with the German Lutherans who became his opponents. Of special interest is the decade of complicated correspondence between Calvin and Zwingli's successor in Zurich, Heinrich Bullinger. Their numerous letters, exchanged treatises, and occasional visits involved far more than the bilateral doctrinal details emphasized below. Dialogue with other theologians and cities, individual loyalties and suspicions, personality differences, pastoral concerns, and especially the military threat of the Counter-Reformation all played significant roles in these negotiations.[1]

The unsuccessful Marburg colloquy (1529) of Luther and Melanchthon with Zwingli and Oecolampadius was followed by relative calm in the doctrinal dispute among the Reformers over the Lord's Supper. The Wittenberg Concord and the First Helvetic Confession, both in 1536, produced some optimism for wider agreement. Calvin's lifelong effort to unite the Reformers in a common doctrine on the Lord's Supper was born in this climate of hope.[2]

---

[1] The negotiations between Calvin and Bullinger are discussed by Hans Grass, *Die Abendmahlslehre bei Luther und Calvin*, 2nd ed., (Gütersloh: C. Bertelsmann, 1954), 208-212, 275-278; Otto Erich Strasser, 'Der Consensus Tigurinus', *Zwingliana* 9/1 (1949): 1-16; Ulrich Gaebler, 'Das Zustandekommen des Consensus Tigurinus im Jahre 1549,' *Theologische Literaturzeitung* 104/5 (1979): 321-332, and 'Consensus Tigurinus,' *Theologische Realenzyklopädie* 8 (1981): 189-192; and Andre Bouvier, *Henri Bullinger le successeur de Zwingli* (Paris: E. Droz, 1940), 110-149 and 471-476. The specific contributions of other secondary literature will be noted in passing. I wish to thank Dr. E. A. Dowey of Princeton Theological Seminary, who first stimulated my interest in this topic during his doctoral seminar on Calvin and Bullinger in the spring of 1976, and Dr. John Burkhart of McCormick Theological Seminary, who generously consented to provide a thorough critique when this paper was the topic of a joint faculty colloquy.

[2] On Calvin's doctrine of the Lord's Supper, see Brian A. Gerrish's excellent bibliography and discussion in 'Gospel and Eucharist: John Calvin on the Lord's Supper,' *The Old Protestantism and the New, Essays on the Reformation Heritage* (Chicago: University of Chicago Press, 1982), 106-117. This chapter is a substantial revision of 'John Calvin and the Reformed Doctrine of the Lord's Supper,' *Una Sancta* 25/2: 27-39. Chapters two and seven of this collection of essays are also cited below, notes 8, 104 and 186. On Calvin's irenic position, see Joseph N. Tylenda, 'The Ecumenical Intention of Calvin's Early Eucharistic Teaching,' *Reformatio Perennis*, ed. Brian A. Gerrish (Pittsburgh: Pickwick Press, 1981), 27-47.

To Calvin, Marburg was not a presupposition for the present, but the regrettable misfortune of an earlier age, before he himself was even committed to the Evangelical cause. His *Short Treatise on the Lord's Supper* in 1541 lamented this 'unhappy business' and attempted an irenic middle course between Luther and Zwingli.[1] The treatise assumes that the Reformers were united in opposing the Papists' error regarding sacrifice, and goes on to face the unfortunate reality of their own divisions over the relationship of the sacramental bread and wine to Christ's body and blood. Before mentioning Luther and Zwingli[1], Calvin previews their controversy with a very specific Christological methodology:

> 'The sacraments of the Lord should not and cannot be at all separated from their reality and substance. To distinguish them so that they be not confused is not only good and reasonable but wholly necessary. But to divide them so as to set them up the one without the other is absurd.'[2]

The implication here is that the Lutheran error was a Monophysite mixture or confusion of sacramental bread and the substance of Christ's body, whereas the Zwinglian error was their Nestorian separation. Like the Chalcedonian Christological formula of the fifth century, Calvin charts a middle course between the mixture of what should be kept distinguished and the separation of what should be kept connected. In this case, bread and body are neither confused nor separated. Calvin here omits the explicit charges of Christological heresy exchanged between Luther and Zwingli, and later between himself and the Lutherans, namely that the Lutheran notion of Christ's bodily omnipresence (ubiquity) confused Christ's divine and human natures and that the Reformed insistence on Christ's body remaining in heaven separated his divine and human natures.

In this treatise, Calvin is primarily concerned not with the relation of Christ's divine and human natures, but with the relation of the sacramental sign to the divine reality, namely neither a confusion nor a separation. Luther, he wrote, should have been clearer 'that he did not intend to set up such a local presence as the Papists imagine.'[3] The error of local or corporeal presence confuses the bread with Christ's body and leads to idolatry and superstition. Thus Calvin opposes any local or corporeal presence of Christ's body. Zwingli and Oecolampadius, on the other hand, opposed such idolatry so single-mindedly 'that they laboured more to destroy the evil than to build up the good,'[4] namely, the reality that *is*

---

[1] *Short Treatise on the Holy Supper of our Lord and only Saviour Jesus Christ* in *Calvin: Theological Treatises*, tr. J. K. S. Reid (Philadelphia: The Westminster Press, 1954), 163. This treatise was also translated by Henry Beveridge in *Tracts and Treatises*, 3 vols, (1844; reprint ed., Grand Rapids, Mich.: Eerdmans, 1958), vol. 2, 194. *Corpus Reformatorum* 33, 457. Henceforth, CR. The *Short Treatise* was written in 1540, and published in 1541.

[2] *Short Treatise*, 147f.; Beveridge, 172. 'Les Sacremens du Seigneur ne se doivent et ne peuvent nullement estre separez de leur verité et substance. De les distinguer a ce qu'on ne les confunde pas, non seulement il est bon et raisonnable, mais du tout necessaire. Et les diviser pour constituer l'un sans l'autre, il n'y a ordre.' CR 33: 439.

[3] *Ibid*, 165; Beveridge, 196; CR 33: 459.

[4] *Ibid*.

conjoined to the sacrament, that through the sacrament we are granted full communion with Christ's body and blood. The Swiss come in for more criticism than the Germans: 'they forgot to define what is the presence of Christ in the Supper in which one ought to believe, and what communication of his body and blood one there receives.'[1] In conclusion, he proposes a union formula more congenial to Lutherans than to Zwinglians, 'we are truly made partakers of the real [proper] substance of the body and blood of Jesus Christ.'[2]

The two positions of this 1541 *Short Treatise*—in favour of a full sacramental communion with Christ's body and blood and yet against their local or corporeal presence—characterized Calvin's sacramental theology throughout his works for the rest of his career Calvin also knew that these positions seemed incompatible. His complicated resolution of this apparent dilemma is also previewed in this treatise, although only in passing, namely, the liturgical words *Sursum corda*: 'lift up your hearts.' The believer enjoys a full communion with Christ's body and blood, even though they are not locally present, 'because we must, to shut out all carnal fancies, raise our hearts on high to heaven, not thinking that our Lord Jesus Christ is so abased as to be enclosed under any corruptible elements.'[3]

After the negotiations within Switzerland during the 1540s, Calvin's *sursum corda* solution became a major point of debate with Luther's followers in the 1550s, led by Joachim Westphal of Hamburg. Meanwhile, the first order of business was the discussion with Zwingli's successor, Heinrich Bullinger, over the first of the two central positions, namely, whether the sacrament was an instrument for full communion with Christ's body and blood. Was the sacrament, in other words, a means of grace? Only a more thorough presentation of Calvin's two complementary positions can lay the groundwork to ask that question, and to assess its eventual answer.

Calvin's clear emphasis on a full communion with Christ by means of the sacrament dominated his writings throughout his life, whether private correspondence or his published works of polemical, pedagogical, and liturgical purposes. The note is sounded early on, in this same *Short Treatise*: the bread and the wine are 'as instruments by which our Lord Jesus Christ distributes them [his body and blood] to us.'[4] This 'instrumentality' is confirmed throughout Calvin's works, as discussed below.

---

[1] *Ibid*; Beveridge, 195; CR 33: 458. The general, Chalcedonian rule of 'distinguish, but do not separate' pervades Calvin's thought, as discussed in Jill Raitt, 'Three Inter-related Principles in Calvin's Unique Doctrine of Infant Baptism,' *Sixteenth Century Journal* 11 (1980): 51-61. I owe this reference to the kindness of Professor John Burkhart.

[2] *Ibid*, 166; Beveridge, 197. 'Nous sommes vrayment faictz participans de la propre substance du corps et du sang de Iesus Christ.' CR 33: 460. On Calvin's consistently positive assessment of Luther, see Brian Gerrish, 'The Pathfinder: Calvin's Image of Martin Luther,' *The Old Protestantism and the New* (see note 2 on p.5, above), 27-48.

[3] *Ibid*, 166; Beveridge, 197f. 'Il nous fault, pour exclurre toutes phantasies charnelles, eslever les cueurs en hault au ciel, ne pensant pas que le Seigneur Iesus soit abaissé iusque là, de estre enclos soubs quelques elemens corruptibles.' CR 33: 460.

[4] *Ibid*, 171 '. . . . pource que ce sont comme instrumens par lesquelz le Seigneur Iesus nous les destribue.' CR 33: 439.

Calvin understood this communion to be not just with Christ's spirit or merely a reception of his benefits.[1] Starting with certain passages in John 6, so disputed by Luther and Zwingli, Calvin affirmed a full participation in Christ's flesh, 'a true and substantial partaking of the body and blood of the Lord.'[2] Both early and late in his career, the French Reformer held to this communion with the whole Christ in the Lord's Supper, in both his divine and human natures. He went to great lengths to express the fullness and completeness of a communion not only with the virtue or power of Christ, but with Christ's very body and blood. He drew the line only at a transfusion or mixture of substance or natures.[3] This emphasis is incomprehensible apart from Calvin's soteriological investment in this communion, since redemption and the whole safety of the believer depend upon it.[4]

Such full communion was possible only through the Holy Spirit. Calvin rarely fails to credit the precise mode of communion to the secret working, the secret influence or virtue of the Holy Spirit, understood as the Spirit of Christ.[5] He closed his *Short Treatise* with this characteristic comment: 'The Spirit of God is the bond of participation, for which reason it is called spiritual.'[6] Although the body of Jesus is in heaven, the Holy Spirit acts as a 'channel,' overcomes the barrier of space, and causes the communion of the faithful with the body and blood of Christ.[7] Calvin's elaboration of this spiritual victory over space—the *sursum corda*—became widely shared in the Reformed tradition, but suspect to the Lutherans.

To Calvin, the denial of the corporeal presence of Christ's body applied to both the Roman Catholic doctrine of transubstantiation and the Lutheran doctrine of ubiquity.[8] He admonished Luther for not rejecting local presence clearly enough and eventually attacked Luther's followers for perpetrating the error of

---

[1] 'Confession of Faith concerning the Eucharist,' *Calvin: Theological Treatises*, edited J. K. S. Reid, (Philadelphia, 1954), 168; 'The Best Method of Obtaining Concord,' *Tracts and Treatises* II, 578.

[2] ... veram substantialemque corporis ac sanguinis Domini communicationem. *Institutio Christianae Religionis 1559*, in Calvin's *Opera Selecta*, ed. Petrus Barth and Guilelmus Niesel (Munich: Kaiser, 1928-1936); Vols. 3-5. IV,17,19. See also the English edition by John T. McNeill and Ford Lewis *Battles* (Philadelphia: Westminster, 1960). Henceforth, *Institutes*.

[3] John Calvin, 'Two Discourses on the Lausanne Articles,' *Theological Treatises,*' 44 and 49; and *Short Treatise*, 146; *Institutes* IV,17,32.

[4] *Institutes* IV,17,11.

[5] *Institutes*, IV,17,31; *Commentary on Corinthians* (Grand Rapids, 1948), I, 300.

[6] *Short Treatise*, 166; Beveridge, 198; CR 33: 460. Cf. *Institutes* IV,14,9 and IV,17,9,12,30 and 33. This was a frequent theme against Westphal in the two treatises mentioned in their context below. They were translated by H. Beveridge in *Tracts and Treatises* II (repr. Grand Rapids: Eerdmans, 1958) as 'Second Defence,' 249, 285, 291, 299, and 306, and 'Last Admonition,' 384, 386, 414, 421, and 445; see also 'The True Partaking of the Flesh and Blood of Christ in the Holy Supper,' *Tracts and Treatises* II, 518.

[7] *Institutes* IV,17,10 and 12.

[8] *Institutes* IV,17,12, 17 and 19; 'Second Defense', 277 and 299.

transubstantiation within the doctrine of ubiquity.[1] Thus Calvin can use the same set of arguments in countering the local presence taught by Roman Catholicism as he did in opposing the 'real' presence of the Lutheran doctrine of ubiquity. Such a presence, often called 'corporeal,' was rejected by Calvin on at least four grounds.

Most frequently mentioned is the danger of a superstitious idolatry of the bread. Calvin wrote to both Roman and Lutheran opponents that the adoration of the bread was not to be tolerated, for it detracts from the worship due to God alone.[2] Early in his career, even during his most irenic period, Calvin viewed this superstitious adoration as worthy of strong and polemical rejection. Writing his colleague Farel regarding the 1541 Diet of Regensburg, an important meeting with Roman Catholic theologians, Calvin reports,

> 'I condemned that peculiar local presence; the act of adoration I declared to
> be altogether insufferable. Believe me, in matters of this kind, boldness is
> absolutely necessary for strengthening and confirming others.'[3]

Years later, he directed to the Lutherans this same spirited denial of the yoked evils, corporeal presence and idolatry:

> 'We not only deny the corporeal presence for the purpose of discountenanc-
> ing the idolatry; but, the better to make it manifest how detestable the fic-
> tion of a corporeal presence is, we show that it necessarily carries an impious
> idolatry along with it.'[4]

Calvin once accused Luther of adoring the sacrament, often called his Lutheran opponents 'bread worshippers,' and condemned such practices as the elevation of the bread (which the Lutherans retained temporarily) or kneeling before the sacrament as ignorant superstitions and idolatry.[5]

Secondly, correct and catholic Christology was Calvin's central objection to a corporeal presence of Christ in the bread. Christ has ascended in his glorified body, which remains in heaven, since it is still circumscribed.[6] Corporeal presence offends both Christ's heavenly glory, by subjecting him to enclosure, and also his human nature, by making him a 'phantasm' or 'apparition.'[7] The role of mediator, so important to Calvin's soteriological Christology, demanded both a fully divine nature and a fully human nature.[8] At stake also was the final resurrection of the dead, for this eschatological event depends upon a true

---

[1] *Institutes* IV,17,16-19 and 30; 'Second Defence,' 282; 'Last Admonition,' 382ff., 387, 413, 454, and 471.

[2] *Institutes,* IV,14,12 and 14; IV,17,13, 20, and 35f. See also Carlos Eire, *War Against Idols: The Reformation of Worship from Erasmus to Calvin* (Cambridge: Cambridge University Press, 1986).

[3] 11 May 1541, CR39: 216; *Letters of John Calvin,* ed. Jules Bonnet (repr. Lenox Hill, 1972), three volumes. I: 261. Henceforth, Bonnet.

[4] CR 37: 231; 'Last Admonition,' 468.

[5] *Ibid;* CR 43: 303 and 488f.; Bonnet III, 91 and 157f.

[6] *Commentary on Acts* (Grand Rapids: Eerdmans, 1949), I, 51.

[7] *Institutes* IV,17,17 and 32; *Short Treatise,* 158.

[8] *Short Treatise,* 158f.; 'Two Discourses,' 42f.; 'Confession of Faith,' 168; 'The Catechism of the Church of Geneva,' 138; 'Second Defence,' 249, 285f., 295 and 299; 'Last Admonition,' 382ff., 387ff., 401; *Institutes* IV,17,18 and 26.

resurrection and ascension of Christ. Because the believers will be like Christ, Calvin argued from the absurdity of the ubiquity of each resurrected believer to a denial of the ubiquity of Christ's body.[1] A blunt caricature of this argument was set forward by the Magdeburg Lutherans, and accepted by Calvin as basically correct:

> 'Scripture declares that our bodies will be made conformable to the glorious body of Christ; but our bodies will not then be everywhere; therefore, neither is the body of Christ everywhere.'[2]

Here the theological motive is in maintaining the humanity of Christ; the religious motive is the hope of the resurrection.

Maintaining a full humanity meant for Calvin that the properties of one nature are not communicable to the other. Specifically the property of omnipresence cannot be communicated from the divine nature to the human nature. Calvin marshals biblical and credal support to oppose this particular type of *communicatio idiomatum* (communication of attributes), later specified as the *genus majestaticum,* as basically Eutychian or confusing the divine and the human nature. Christ's body remains therefore a truly human, i.e. spatially defined, body.

> 'But it is the nature of a body to be contained in space, to have its own dimensions and its own shape. Away, then, with this stupid fiction which fastens both men's minds and Christ to bread!'[3]

In the third place, the idea of a corporeal presence is objectionable because it is an offence to the Holy Spirit. This objection takes two forms. First, the vital role of Christ's spirit in binding the believers to Christ makes corporeal presence unnecessary; thus to insist on it is to offend the proper work of the Spirit.

> 'Yet a serious wrong is done to the Holy Spirit, unless we believe that it is through his incomprehensible power that we come to partake of Christ's flesh and blood.'[4]

Further, if Christ's body is locally or ubiquitously present, unbelievers would partake of Christ without the simultaneous working of the Spirit. This is intolerable to Calvin not only because communion with Christ is salvation and thus unavailable without faith, but also because Christ and his Spirit cannot be separated.

> 'By what right do they allow themselves to dissever Christ from his Spirit? This we account nefarious sacrilege. They insist that Christ is received by the wicked, to whom they do not concede one particle of the Spirit of Christ.'[5]

---

[1] *Institutes* IV,17,29.
[2] 'Last Admonition,' 458. CR 37: 224. Cf. 'Second Defence,' 280 and 289; 'Last Admonition,' 290f., 'Two Articles,' 43.
[3] *Institutes* IV,17,29.
[4] *Institutes* IV,17,33; cf. 'Second Defence,' 285, 306; 'Last Admonition,' 411.
[5] This quotation comes from Calvin's (first) *Defensio* of the *Consensus Tigurinus* (CR 37: 27), 'Exposition,' *Tracts and Treatises* II, 234. See Jill Raitt's article, cited in note 1 on p.7 above.

In this case, Calvin explicitly opposed the Lutherans, who maintained that Christ was present in the bread and wine whether or not the Spirit had yet worked faith in the recipient. This viewpoint entailed the *manducatio indignorum*, the 'eating by the unworthy', a point of contention between Reformed and Lutheran views of Christ's presence in the Supper for centuries.

In the fourth place, the idea of corporeal presence contradicts the very definition of a sacrament. 'The matter [res] must always be distinguished from the sign, that we may not transfer to the one what belongs to the other.'[1] If the flesh of Christ were physically present under the form of bread, the relationship between the sign and the thing [res] would be reduced to one of identity. The sign would *be* the thing, and the nature of a sacrament would be violated.[2] Furthermore, the idea of a corporeal presence completely changes the nature of the sacramental mystery. In transubstantiation, the metaphysical change is the miracle, whereas the subsequent communion is quite reasonable, since the believers consume the very substance of Christ's flesh and are thus corporeally united to him. In Calvin's emphasis, the metaphysical dimension is unremarkable, since bread remains bread, but the miraculous mystery (incredible, sweet, and wonderful)[3] is the personal communion. This mystery, the mode of communion that overcomes space, involves the *Sursum corda*, mentioned above and discussed more fully below.

In conclusion, both his affirmation of full communion with Christ and his denial of the corporeal presence of Christ in the bread influenced Calvin's negative answer to the controversial question: Do unbelievers receive the body and blood of Christ? The denial of corporeal presence permitted a negative answer, since Christ was not corporeally present for all to consume. The affirmation of full communion, in Calvin's terms, *required* a negative answer, since communion with Christ was the source of redemption, not enjoyed by unbelievers, whether they ate and drank bread and wine or not.[4]

To summarize, Calvin took a Chalcedonian *via media*, affirming the sacrament as a means of full communion with Christ's body and blood over against the Zwinglian separation of sacramental sign and reality, and rejecting a corporeal presence of Christ over against the Lutherans' closer identification of the sign and the thing itself, Christ's body. Calvin spent the first decade after his *Short Treatise*, from 1540 to 1549, negotiating this first point with Heinrich Bullinger in Zurich. Thereafter, in the 1550s, he was embroiled in disputes with Luther's followers Joachim Westphal and others, not so much over the second point, the rejection of a corporeal presence, as over Calvin's reconciliation of the two positions through the *sursum corda*, that the believers are lifted up by the Holy Spirit to commune with Christ's body and blood at the right hand of the *Father*.

---

[1] *Institutes* IV,14,15.
[2] Cf. Heiko A. Oberman, 'The "Extra" Dimension' in the Theology of Calvin, *Journal of Ecclesiastical History* 21 (1970): 43ff.
[3] *Commentary on Corinthians* I, 380.
[4] *Institutes* IV,17,11.

## HEINRICH BULLINGER

When Calvin interacted with Zurich, he knew that he was negotiating not with Zwingli's memory or a static Zwinglian legacy, but with a prodigious scholar and independent leader, one whose accomplishments could not be overlooked in the sixteenth century and should not be under-estimated today. Heinrich Bullinger (1504-1575) not only authored the decisive *Second Helvetic Confession* of 1566 and influenced 'covenant theology'; through works such as *The Decades* and his voluminous correspondence, and through his hospitality to Protestant refugees, he also exerted a broad influence upon the Reformed tradition generally, and especially upon the Elizabethan clergy in England. Bullinger's significance is currently under careful examination as his immense corpus of over one hundred books and 15,000 letters receives its long overdue critical edition and scholarly review.[1]

Heinrich Bullinger was born near Zurich in July of 1504, the fifth son of the parish priest in Bremgarten, who lived faithfully and openly with his partner Anna. While their precocious son Heinrich was away at school in Emmerich and Cologne, father Bullinger opposed a local indulgence hawker in 1519, much as Luther had countered Tetzel. Filled with enthusiasm for the Fathers and the New Testament, convinced of the Evangelical cause by reading and discussing Luther and Melanchthon in Cologne in 1520-22, young Bullinger returned from his studies to a Reform-minded family and community. He continued his research, taught, and wrote substantial works of Reformation theology, all before ever meeting Ulrich Zwingli. They first met in 1524 when their initial topic of conversation was, in fact, the Lord's Supper, as pursued below. The overall impression was favorable, and mutual. In 1529, Bullinger became the pastor in his home town of Bremgarten. He succeeded his own father, who officially turned Protestant, received a Christian blessing on his thirty-year marriage, and retired. In order to concentrate on parish ministry, Bullinger declined Zwingli's invitation

---

[1] *Heinrich Bullinger Werke*, ed. Fritz Büsser (Zurich: Theologisher Verlag, 1972-). The first two volumes were bibliographies: Joachim Staedtke, *Beschreibendes Verzeichnis der gedruckten Werke von Heinrich Bullinger* (1972), and Erland Herkenrath, *Beschreibendes Verzeichnis der Literatur uber Heinrich Bullinger* (1977). The first volumes of Bullinger's edited works are devoted to his enormous correspondence, with three volumes required to reach 1533, and to early exegetical works. For a large collection of articles, see the two volumes edited by Ulrich Gabler and Erland Herkenrath, *Heinrich Bullinger, 1504-1575. Gesammelte Aufsätze zum 400. Todestag* (Zurich: Theologischer Verlag, 1975); *Erster Band: Leben und Werk, Zweiter Band: Beziehungen und Wirkungen* (*Zürcher Beiträge zur Reformationsgeschichte*, 7-8). Henceforth, *Heinrich Bullinger 1504-1575*. For an indication of the current rising estimations of Bullinger's importance, see Fritz Büsser, 'Bullinger, Heinrich (1504-1575),' *Theologische Realenzyklopädie* 7 (1981): 375-387. See also Wayne Baker, *Bullinger and the Covenant* (Columbus: Ohio University Press, 1981). For an example of the new work on Bullinger, see Mark S. Burrows, ' "Christus intra nos vivens." The Peculiar Genius of Bullinger's Doctrine of Sanctification,' *Zeitschrift fur Kirchengeschichte* 98 (1987): 48-69.

to go with him to Marburg later that year, although they had attended the Bern disputation together in 1528.[1]

Current scholarship is clarifying the background of Bullinger's views on the Lord's Supper, well before he entered negotiations with Calvin in the 1540s, and indeed even before he discussed the subject with Zwingli in 1524. Like Calvin, Bullinger is often treated as a second-generation Reformer since he was, as his main biographer put it, *Henri Bullinger, le successeur de Zwingli*.[1] Yet Bullinger's own student experience in Cologne from 1519, his encounter there with Luther's thought, and his own numerous writings of the 1520s certainly place him closer to the beginnings of the Reformation than to a second generation. As with other first-generation Reformers, his own initial agenda on this topic included *de origine erroris, in negocio eucharistiae, ac missae* (1528), one of his earliest extant published works.[2] The error of the Mass is the medieval misunderstanding of what the early church Fathers meant by 'sacrifice.' The only acceptable offering, summarized Bullinger years later, was the sacrifice of prayerful remembrance and thanksgiving for gifts already received.[3]

The early Bullinger was deeply influenced by Luther's works in general and by the category of 'testament' in particular. A separate and major study would be needed to evaluate Bullinger's incorporation of Luther's testament motif into his own covenant theology which so influenced Reformed theology and especially Puritan thought. But crucial for the current purpose is Bullinger's 1520/21 reading of Luther's *Babylonian Captivity*, his decision that Luther was right and the scholastics were wrong, and his use of the testament motif to characterize the Lord's Supper both early and late in his life. In a 1526 letter, he wrote:

'Briefly, the testament is the blessing or forgiveness of sins, Christ is the mediator of the testament, the dead body and the blood of Christ are truly the revealing and the sealing of the testament, the bread and wine are the symbols of the confirmed testament, which remind [us] of redemption and union.'[4]

Later on, in the *Decades* (five groups of ten essays each, in the form of sermons), Bullinger adds that Christians are the heirs, and that the inheritance attested in

---

[1] For Bullinger's general theological development up to this point, see Fritz Blanke, *Der junge Bullinger* (Zurich: Zwingli Verlag, 1942) and Joachim Staedtke, *Die Theologie des jungen Bullinger* (Zurich: Zwingli Verlag, 1962). Much of Bullinger's life and work is also reflected in a fragmentary way in his own *Diarium (Annales Vitae) der Jahre 1504-1574* (Basel: Basler Buch- und Antiquariatshandlung, 1904), including the appended autobiographical sketch (pp. 125ff.). Henceforth, *Diary*.

[2] Andre Bouvier, *Henri Bullinger, le successeur de Zwingli* (Paris: E. Droz, 1940). See also Carl Pestalozzi, *Heinrich Bullinger, Leben und ausgewählte Schriften* (Elberfeld, 1858). Both of these biographical works will likely be superseded soon by a modern biography based upon the current editing of Bullinger's works. A good sketch of Bullinger's life and thought is provided by Robert C. Walton, 'Heinrich Bullinger 1504-1575' in *Shapers of Religious Traditions in Germany, Switzerland, and Poland 1560-1600*, edited Jill Raitt (New Haven: Yale University Press, 1981), 69-87.

[3] See the Staedtke bibliography (note 1 on p.12, above), 7-13

[4] *Ein predig von den rechten Opfferen der Christenheit* (Aug. 13, 1552), 4 and 25f. On microfilm at Speer Library, Princeton Theological Seminary.

this last will and testament is the forgiveness of sins.[1] (Of course, Luther believed the Supper not only to attest to forgiveness, but also to convey it.)

But Luther's influence on the very young Bullinger was actually secondary to that of other pre-Reformers. The teenager's conversion to the Evangelical cause in Cologne in 1521 hinged on a rejection of transubstantiation and a new understanding of the Lord's Supper, based on his reading, it seems, of certain Waldensians and Wessel Gansfort.

When Bullinger and Zwingli met in 1524, the twenty-year-old prodigy confronted the established Reformer with an independent view of the Lord's Supper, one which gave Zwingli pause. Bullinger wrote in his diary,

> On September 12th, Zwingli shared his thoughts with me, how he viewed the sacrament of the body and blood of the Lord. And I in good faith expounded to him my views, which I drew from the writings of the Waldensian brethren and the books of Augustine.[1]

Notice that Bullinger is clear that he had independent sources for his thought, and that the meeting was a true exchange of views, not a young man being influenced by his elder. In a ground-breaking study, Hans Georg vom Berg has uncovered some of the background of Bullinger's views on the Lord's Supper *before* this meeting with Zwingli.[1] Vom Berg investigates the avenues of influence which the Waldensian tradition, including the Bohemian Brethren, could have had on Bullinger in Cologne. When Wessel Gansfort's writings are also considered, a striking picture emerges of Bullinger's independence from and even opposition to Zwingli from the very beginning. Through this tradition, Bullinger came independently to a 'symbolic' view of the Lord's Supper, that the words 'This is my body' really mean 'This signifies my body.' This much Zwingli and his correspondent, Cornelius Hoen, certainly found agreeable. But, argues vom Berg, on another point Bullinger followed Wessel Gansfort in sharp contrast to Zwingli and Hoen:

> The subject in the Lord's Supper is not, as in Zwingli and Hoen, the faithful or the congregation, but the present Christ who gives himself as he gave himself up in his passion, and therewith unites God's love and eternal life as closely and as thoroughly as iron and fire are bound together.... The Lord's Supper is not only a rite of thanksgiving and remembrance, in which the congregation re-presents in faith the gracious offering of Christ, but also a sacramental act of dedication and re-presentation, still a spiritual commemoration in faith, *but* such that the faithful remembering congregation

---

[1] Bullinger and Enzlin to Christoph Stiltz, 27 Feb. 1526, *Heinrich Bullinger Werke*, Briefwechsel I, 111. Staedtke, *Der junge Bullinger*, 251.

[2] *The Decades*, Heinrich Bullinger, tr. Thomas Harding (Cambridge, 1849-52), V,9,403. Henceforth, *Decades*. See also Ulrich Gäbler, 'Der junge Bullinger und Luther,' *Lutherjahrbuch* (1975): 131-140. On Bullinger's overall relationship with Luther and Lutherans, see Wilhelm A. Schulze, 'Bullingers Stellung zum Luthertum,' *Heinrich Bullinger 1504-1575* II: 287-314.

[3] *Diary*, 9, 11ff.

has the passive, receptive role, and the self-giving Christ is alone the active subject.[1]

Zwingli's views of the Supper as the congregation's symbolic commemoration were still in formation during this 1524 meeting with Bullinger. He had just received a crucial letter from Hoen on the subject. Perhaps, contrary to the prevailing view of Bullinger as Zwingli's uncritical heir, the elder here learned something from the younger, who had already pursued the subject for several years. Zwingli asked Bullinger not to publish his views or their differences; he would do it himself at the right time.[2] Zwingli's views of a symbolic Lord's Supper are well-known from later writings and the accounts of the Marburg Colloquy. Generally speaking, he continued the Hoen line of the Supper as the congregation's commemoration and testimonial to faith. Bullinger's (and Wessel's) view that the active subject is not the congregation but Christ remained a point of difference between them. Yet late in his brief life, Zwingli did pursue a complicated Platonic understanding of remembrance, as Gottfried Locher has shown, in which the active subject is not so much the believers who remember the past but God who reminds them of it in the present. Again, in some late writings such as *Fidei ratio* (1530) and *Fidei expositio* (1531), Zwingli also referred to the sacrament as a perceptible analogy for grace. Yet for Zwingli this analogy is the congregation's visual aid for the simple beginner rather than as God's own testimony and confirmation of grace.[3] As will become apparent, Bullinger shared several of Zwingli's concerns, especially the urgent prohibition of any superstitious use of the sacrament. With Zwingli, he also denied that God is bound to the sacrament and that it confers grace.

Nevertheless, beyond these common denials, Bullinger made much more pointed affirmations about the sacraments as God's way of testifying and confirming the Spirit's work on the heart. His contrasting and prior view of the Lord's Supper as something *God* does is crucial. The primary activity in the Supper, for Bullinger, is not that of the congregation, remembering and testifying to the faith, but that of God who by a visual analogy testifies to the redemption accomplished in Christ's body and blood.[4] Grammatically and theologically, the believer is not the subject, but rather the direct or indirect object of this activity, as Bullinger summarized much later:

'The supper of the Lord is an holy action instituted unto the church from God, wherein the Lord, by the setting of bread and wine before us at the banquet, doth certify unto us his promise and communion, and sheweth unto us his gifts, and layeth them before our senses.'[5]

---

[1] 'Spätmittelalterliche Einflusse auf die Abendmahlslehre des jungen Bullinger,' *Kerygma und Dogma* 22 (1976): 221-233. See also Walton's (undocumented) assertion that Bullinger refused to attend Mass as early as 1522 (note 2 on p.13 above).

[2] vom Berg, 231 and 233.

[3] vom Berg, 222.

[4] Gottfried Locher, *Huldrych Zwingli in Neuer Sicht* (Zurich: Zwingli Verlag, 1968), 251-259 and *Zwingli's Thought, New Perspectives* (Leiden: Brill, 1981), 214-228 and 314-326. See also Locher's appreciation for Bullinger in 277-287, and in 'Heinrich Bullinger und der Spätzwinglianismus,' *Die Zwinglische Reformation* (Göettingen: Vandenhoeck & Ruprecht, 1979), 584-605, and 613f.

[5] *Decades*, V,9,403; cf. V,6,240, V,7,316f., 327, and V,9,443.

Bullinger's differences with Zwingli on this crucial point, to anticipate the discussion below, did not result from Calvin's persuasive arguments in the 1540s, as many interpreters of their correspondence imply, but date rather from the very beginnings of Bullinger's own thought, before he even met Zwingli, much less fell under his shadow.

That shadow fell on Bullinger not so much through Zwingli's life and work as through his death and near-elevation to martyrdom by the Zurichers. When Zwingli died in the Protestant military defeat at Cappel in 1531, the Evangelical cause in and around Zurich was badly shaken. Roman Catholic opponents seized the occasion to interpret the fall of Zwingli and the Zurichers as divine judgment on his heresies. The other clergy and lay leaders of Zurich needed a head pastor who would live up to high standards of biblical scholarship and preaching, and would also lead their recovery of confidence by defending Zwingli and the Zurich Reformation from such attacks. Bullinger turned down overtures from Basel and Bern, but accepted the duties of head pastor (*antistes*) of the Zurich congregation, which he faithfully pursued for forty-four years. Only twenty-seven years old, he was already the author of almost one hundred theological and exegetical works, most of them never published and/or lost.

Yet all of this independent scholarship faded before his first and abiding pastoral challenge: to rally the spirits of the Zurichers by defending their tradition and their martyred leader from attack. Immediately upon taking office, Bullinger wrote such a defence against Faber, the leading Roman Catholic apologist who had credited the Catholic military victory at Cappel to their true faith, and the Protestant defeat to their heresy. In his response, Bullinger reveals his lifelong aversion to controversies and also a willingness to suppress the independence of his thought, including that of his sacramental theology discussed above, in order to defend Zwingli fully. Bullinger challenges the very idea that military victory or defeat defines the faith as true or false. Faber had in fact charged that the Protestant defeat grew from their belittling of the sacraments.[1] At this point it was pastorally imperative to defend Zwingli's sacramental theology and thus the Zurich tradition with every possible argument, and to pass by discreetly any differences that Bullinger may have had with his predecessor. For a dozen years and more, it was part of the Zurichers' self-understanding and thus part of Bullinger's pastoral duty to uphold Zwingli's memory and his memorial theology as almost that of a prophet and a martyr of the faith. His narrative of Zwingli's life and death is close to hagiography.[2] Bullinger's investment may have been more than pastoral; according to the traditional account he took Zwingli's widow and two children into his own home as part of his large

---

[1] *Uff Johansen Wyenischen Bischoff's Trostbuchlein* (Zurich, 1532), especially page 9. On microfilm at Union Theological Seminary.

[2] Regarding Zwingli, Bullinger's *Reformation History* is excerpted in G. R. Potter, *Huldrych Zwingli* (New York: St. Martin's Press, 1977). See also Ulrich Gäbler, *Huldrych Zwingli. His Life and Work*, English translation by Ruth C. L. Gritsch (Philadelphia: Fortress, 1986), 155-160.

extended family.[1] Only gradually and under another military necessity did Bullinger reveal his original points of difference with Zwingli, which made dialogue with John Calvin possible and eventually fruitful.

In this dialogue Calvin repeatedly took the initiative, pressing for a meeting with Bullinger in which they could affirm the unity of the church in Geneva and Zurich. Calvin's desire for explicit unity was based on his theological confession of one church and his pastoral concern to reassure those ministers and lay people who were unsettled by the absence of formal agreement between Geneva and Zurich.[2] He wrote to Bullinger in 1539:

'We see indeed of how much importance that is, not only on our account, but for the sake of the whole body of professing Christians everywhere, that all those on whom the Lord has laid any personal charge in the ordering of His Church, should agree together in a sincere and cordial understanding.'[3]
Although Calvin was correct in noting some room for negotiations, several facets of Bullinger's situation would delay any serious dialogue for years. First, as discussed above, Bullinger's pastoral duties required an unqualified defense of Zwingli as his congregation's founding father, even against the irenic criticisms of Calvin's *Short Treatise*. Thus he had to treat any critic of Zwingli, even Calvin, with caution. Secondly, Bullinger was receptive to correspondence but less so to direct verbal negotiations. His biographer, Andre Bouvier, writes that Bullinger's caution and tactical preference for consolidating his positions before moving into anything new stood in marked contrast to the eagerness and talent for direct, immediate negotiations which Calvin's training and disposition had given him.[4] Finally, the same event which narrowed Calvin's hopes from that of general Protestant union to only Swiss Protestantism also delayed Bullinger's active involvement with Geneva, namely, Luther's renewed attack on the Zurich position as heretical.

Hints of Luther's views of Schwenckfeld, the *Schwärmer* or Enthusiasts, and the Zwinglians as equally heretical trickled out of Germany in 1541 and 1542. Luther's private letter of August 31, 1543, to Froschauer, the Zurich publisher who had sent him a newly edited Latin Bible, informed the Zurichers that he wanted no more correspondence or writings from them since they and their founders were in error and misleading the faithful.[5] Bullinger and the other Zurich ministers were eager to defend the memory of Zwingli and the integrity of their own faith, but refrained. As Bullinger wrote to a friend, 'If Luther doesn't

---

[1] Bouvier, 27f.; Diary, 37. But see Locher, 'Bullinger und Spätzwinglianismus,' (note 4 on p.15 above), 588.

[2] Calvin to Bullinger, 21 February 1538, CR 37: 153f., Bonnet I, 65-67; as echoed later in the *Defensio*, 244 and the *Second Defence*, 250. As for the general theological comparison and relationship of Calvin and Bullinger, see G. Locher, 'Bullinger und Calvin, Probleme des Vergleichs ihrer Theologien,' *Heinrich Bullinger 1504-1575* II, 1-33.

[3] CR 39: 28 (early 1540); Bonnet I, 113, here dated 12 March 1539.

[4] Bouvier, 127 and 131.

[5] *Luthers Werke*, Weimar Edition, 57 vols. Eds. J. F. K. Knaake *et al.* (Weimar, 1883ff.) Briefwechsel 10: 387. Henceforth, WA.

attack us in print, we will avoid a battle with him.'[1] In republishing Zwingli's works, Zurich continued to identify itself with the object of Luther's attacks, but the public position was that of tolerance. This silence was maintained until Luther's judgment of 'Karlstadt, Zwingli, Oecolampadius, Schwenckfeld and their disciples at Zurich or wherever they may be' as Schwärmer and enemies of the sacrament' did appear in print in his *Brief Confession Concerning the Holy Sacrament* in 1544.[2] Zwingli was, in Luther's invective, 'an enemy of the holy sacrament and a full-blown heathen' and so was anyone else who identified with him.[3]

Calvin recognized the negative impact of such language on church agreement. He wrote Melanchthon about it, and, on another subject, wrote an irenic, respectful letter to Luther addressing him three times as his 'father' in the faith.[4] He also wrote Bullinger pleading with him to remember Luther's 'greatness as a man and outstanding gifts' as a distinguished servant of God, but also knowing that Zurich could not let this rebuke pass without public rebuttal.[5] At the same time, Calvin's correspondence with Bullinger maintained a discreet silence on his recent judgment of Zwingli's contribution as clearly inferior to Luther's, as already hinted in the *Short Treatise*.[6]

Urged on by the city magistrates, Bullinger led the Zurich clergy in a long and detailed response, the *Warhaffte Bekanntnus* (True Confession) of 1545. It denies each charge of heresy, setting out their full confession of faith, including especially regarding the Lord's Supper, and it counter-charges that Luther's position on the sacramental presence of Christ was itself heretical. The work begins on a note of sadness at such disputes within the church, but with resolve to defend the memory of the 'faithful and praiseworthy Zwingli and Oecolampadius.' Even in Bullinger's irenic hands, sixteenth-century polemics are heated.

---

[1] Bullinger to Bucer, 8 August 1543 in Wilhelm Kolfhaus, 'Der Verkehr Calvins mit Bullinger,' *Calvinstudien*, ed. A. Bohatec, (Leipzig: R. Haupt, 1909), 49. Bullinger's respect for Luther, (as in letters WA Br.8, 281 and 546) dates from his Cologne debt to Luther's writings on testament. Since Melanchthon also felt vulnerable to Luther's wrath, Bullinger invited him to seek refuge in Zurich! On Philip's frequent and serious thoughts of exile, before and after the *Consensus Tigurinus*, see Wilhelm H. Neuser, 'Die Versuche Bullingers, Calvins and der Strassburger, Melanchthon zum Fortgang von Wittenberg zu Bewegen,' *Heinrich Bullinger 1504-1575* II, 35-55.

[2] *Kurzes Bekenntnis vom heiligen Sakrament*, WA 54, 141. *Luther's Works*, American Edition, 56 vols. Eds. Pelikan and Lehmann (St. Louis and Philadelphia: Concordia Publishing House and Fortress Press, 1955ff.) 38: 287f. Henceforth LW.

[3] . . . nicht allein ein Feind des heiligen Sacraments, sondern wird auch gantz und gar zum Heiden. WA 54: 143; LW 38: 289-291, 302. In a letter to Jacob Probst dated 17 January 1546 (WA Br. 11:264), Luther bends Psalm 1 to his anti-Zwinglian use: 'Blessed is the man who walks not in the counsel of the sacramentarians, nor stands in the way of Zwinglians, nor sits in the seat of the Zurichers.' See Gerrish, *Old and New*, 33.

[4] Calvin to Melanchthon, CR 39: 698, and CR 40: 10; Calvin to Luther, 21 January 1545, CR 40: 6-8 (Bonnet I, 440).

[5] CR 39: 774f., Bonnet I, 432-434; cf. Bouvier, 130.

[6] CR 39: 24, Bonnet I, 109.

Luther's book, he continues,

> is so full of devils, unchristian expressions, slanderous words, quarrelsome wishes, impure speech, anger, deception, fury and foaming, that all who read it and have not become insane with him, must marvel at great lengths and with amazement at the far-ranging and unbelievable example that such an old, venerable, learned, and respected man can do nothing else than become so badly decayed and confused.[1]

The purpose of Bullinger's book was partly to correct the historical record concerning Zwingli and Marburg, and partly to counter-attack Luther's teaching. But primarily it was to defend the current Zurich view of the Christian faith in general and the Lord's Supper in particular:

> And beyond that, because he scolded our forefathers and us as willingly stubborn and unrepentant heretics who present false and poisonous doctrine to churches, and who lead pious churches into distress, indeed who believe not one piece of Christian faith rightly but especially concerning the holy sacrament of the body and blood of Christ, who last of all initiate, perpetuate, and defend deceptive and unchristian teaching which stands opposed to God's word and ancient christian church doctrine, so we wish to confess and recount freely, truly, briefly, and clearly our teaching and our common faith and in a short sum also the Supper of the Lord Jesus Christ, and with God's help to substantiate clearly and prove that our teaching and faith is Christian and correct, not heretical and false, indeed that it is taken out of the Word of God and is like and in agreement with the holy ancient Christian church teaching.'[2]

The *Warhaffte Bekanntnus* spends some forty detailed pages revisiting Marburg and its aftermath, defending Zwingli and criticizing Luther for his behavior. Another thirty pages set forth their general confession of faith which, contrary to Luther's accusation of total heresy, is the true, scriptural, unambiguous faith 'of Christians, not Zwinglians or Oecolampadians, much less Lutherans.'[3] On the Lord's Supper in particular, the Zurich defense of its tradition maintains that the correct chief article and goal of the Supper is

> 'the remembrance of the sacrificed body and blood shed for the forgiveness of our sins.... For the Lord commanded his faithful to Do: therefore he set forth and ordained an Action, an undertaking and general activity or deed, namely that his faithful should do that which he has done. What? Thanksgiving, breaking bread and eating, distributing drink and drinking. But why? To his remembrance, namely that he was given over to death for us and has shed his blood for the washing of our sins.'[4]

The facet of the service most emphasized was the 'action', which Latin word appears several times in this German text in special capital letters. 'The sign is the

---

[1] *Warhaffte Bekanntnus der dieneren der kirchen zu Zuerych* (Zurich: Froschauer, 1545), 3. On microfilm at Union Theological Seminary. The work was also published in Latin: *Orthodoxa Tigurinae ecclesiae ministrorum confessio* (Zurich: Froschauer, 1545).

[2] *Warhaffte Bekanntnus*, 5.

[3] *Ibid*, 42a.

[4] *Ibid*, 70f.

entirely visible external Action in which the bread is broken and eaten and the drink is poured out and drunk.'[1] These actions stimulate the faithful to remembrance:

'Such a remembrance may not and can not happen correctly and as the Lord commanded without true faith. For that reason the remembrance [gedächtnus] in the Supper is not an empty dream [gedicht]: because faith is no idle dream. . . . The same faith really and truly makes the good things which are gained with the sacrificed body and shed blood of Christ present (to) the faithful. . . . Out of all this it forcefully and undeniably follows that the one who has truly eaten the flesh of Christ and has drunk his blood is the one who believes in Christ, true God and human crucified for us. Thus believing is eating and eating believing.'[2]

This position, expounded at length, carries on the Zwinglian tradition in all its complexity, namely that 'remembrance' is not purely human recalling but also divine reminding. Here Bullinger's emphasis on the sacramental agency of God is consistent with the late Zwingli. In summary,

'the Lord of the church keeps his suffering and our redemption in fresh remembrance in the church so that he might refer to and point out his grace and great gifts, which are received in faith, faith which he exercises through these external acts.'[3]

The rest of the treatise considers various objections, counters Luther's views on a local presence as Scholastic and therefore unreformed, and refutes Luther's other charges of heresy. By way of final conclusion, Zwingli is to be defended but not idealized, since he too was human, while Luther is to be refuted but not harshly condemned, since he too is part of the unity in Christ which the Zurichers were reluctant to undermine. Later, when Luther died, Bullinger wrote that he loved and admired the famous man of blessed memory, 'through whom the Lord conferred splendid benefits on us,' but also that Luther's view of the Supper lacked only the word 'transubstantiation' to be a papist abomination.[4]

## THE FIRST SUBSTANTIVE DIALOGUE

Even as the *Warhaffte Bekanntnus* was circulating, Bullinger wrote another volume on the same subject, his *Absoluta* or *de Sacramentis*, but with several striking contrasts: it was not in German but in Latin, it was initially distributed not

---

[1] 'Das zeichen ist die gantz sichtbar ussere Action in deren das brot gebrochen und geessen des tranck uss gegossen und getruncken wirt.' *Ibid*, 75. Other locations of *Actio* are 74b and 76a.

[2] *Ibid*, 79.

[3] 'Das er in der kirchen sin lyden und unsere erlosung in frisher gedachtnus behielten dazu sin gnad und grosse gaaben uns bezugte und verzeichnete welche durch den glouben empfangen werdend: den glouben aber ubt er mit der usseren handlung.' *Ibid*, 79a.

[4] Bullinger to Thamaerus, 14 November 1546, CR 40:416-418.

widely but privately, it was not a polemical response to Luther but an irenical statement shared with Calvin. Most importantly, it contrasts Bullinger the representative defender of Zurich's Zwingli with Bullinger the independent theologian whose sacramental emphasis was not on the theme of remembrance, Zwinglian or otherwise. His Diary for 1545 opens and closes with these entries:

'At the end of February, I completed the German response given by all the ministers of the Zurich church to Luther. I sent it with cover letters to many princes, cities, and churches.
– – – – – – – – – – – –
'I finished, along with the end of '45, my book on the sacraments of Christ the Lord and the catholic church; it has sixteen chapters. I published this book in another form in two sermons of the fifth *Decade* in 1551. It was printed in its first form in London, England, in 1551, by John a Lasco and dedicated to the queen.'[1]

Here Bullinger himself contrasts the one work as a widely distributed joint response of all the Zurich clergy, with the other as his own personal book on the sacraments which was not publicly available for six years. In the meantime it was shared with Calvin, probably given to him during his visit to Zurich in January of 1547. Calvin's letter in response immediately mirrors Bullinger's apparent concern for confidentiality:

'I read your book as soon as I returned home. The silence you asked of me I have been honouring in utter good faith. Have no doubts. . . . I have long desired, in a strikingly deep way, that we come to an agreement.'[2]

Calvin had thought little of the Zurichers' *Wahrhaffte Bekanntnus*, writing to Melanchthon that the whole booklet was insipid and childish, more stubborn than learned. As late as 1546 Calvin was still hoping to reconcile Luther and Zurich.[3] Thus he welcomed the opportunity for dialogue with Bullinger's less public and polemical side, and responded to his private work in great detail. The *Absoluta*, therefore, and the thorough response to it form the first substantive, direct dialogue between Bullinger and Calvin regarding the Lord's Supper.

A collation of the rare original work as published by a Lasco with the version included in the *Decades* confirms that chapters one to eight constitute the sixth sermon of the fifth *Decade*, with only the slightest editorial adjustments. Even the marginal subheadings seem identical, and only the addition of 'The Lord be

---

[1] *Diary*, 32f. See the Staedtke bibliography, 91, regarding this rare work entitled *Absoluta de Christi Domini et Catholicae eius Ecclesiae Sacramentis*. Of the four known copies, the one consulted for this study is that of Union Theological Seminary, New York.

[2] 25 February 1547, CR 40: 480. This letter (no. 880) is actually a small essay in critique of Bullinger's work (CR 40: 480-489). It is also discussed by Ernst Bizer, *Studien zur Geschichte des Abendmahlsstreits im 16 Jahrhundert*, 2nd edition (Darmstadt, Wissenschaftliche Buchgesellschaft, 1962), 251-256.

[3] 'Praeterquam enim quod totus libellus ieiunus est et puerilis, quum in multis pertinaciter magis quam erudite. 28 June 1545, CR 40: 98. This portion of the letter is not in Bonnet's translation, I, 466. On Calvin's late hopes for reconciliation between Luther and the Zurichers, see CR 40: 316; Bonnet II, 40

praised, Amen' converted the conclusion of these eight chapters into the conclusion of a 'sermon' for the *Decades*. Chapters nine through sixteen, likewise, constitute the seventh sermon, with one major change in chapter eleven, as discussed below. Used in this light, the *Decades* V, 6 and 7 can document Bullinger's own 1545 views on the Lord's Supper, before his negotiations with Calvin. His own editorial changes and the subsequent works written during and after the next five years of complicated negotiations may therefore indicate where his positions were modified and where they were maintained.

The title of *Decade* V, 6 abbreviates and conflates the first eight chapter titles of Bullinger's *Absoluta* as follows, with the original chapter numbers added in brackets:

'[1] Of signs, and the manner of signs; [2] Of sacramental signs: what a sacrament is; [3] Of whom, for what causes, [4] And how many sacraments were instituted of Christ for the Christian church; [5] Of what things they do consist; [6] How these are consecrated; [7] How the sign and the thing signified in the sacraments are either joined together or distinguished; [8] And of the kind of speeches used in the sacraments.'[1]

Bullinger began with a general discussion of signs and then surveyed the various terms used regarding the sacraments. To this (chapter two), Calvin responded that the Greek word 'mysteries' is the best single substitute for the Latin *sacramenta*.[2] Two sacraments were instituted by God, because of divine goodness and human weakness, which occasioned no comment from Calvin. The sacraments consist of the visible sign and the invisible thing signified, but the Lord did not promise to be tied to the signs, argued Bullinger.

'Those words of the Lord ('this is my body, this is my blood') are not rigidly to be expounded according to the letter, as though bread and wine were the body and blood of Christ substantially and corporeally, but symbolically and sacramentally.'[1]

For Bullinger, the 'remembrance' of Christ implied the absence of Christ, whereas Calvin pursued a dialectic of absence and presence. True, replies Calvin, Christ is absent to our eyes, for his body is in heaven.

'But he is present to the faithful through the power of his Spirit, since distance does not hinder Christ from miraculously feeding his own. ... for Christ does not descend to us from heaven, nor is he discerned by the eye. But he is nevertheless present to us in faith.'[1]

---

[1] *Decades* V,6,226. The chapters of the original work correspond to the following pagination in the Parker edition: 1: 227-233 bottom; 2: 233-239 top; 3: 239-246 top; 4: 246-249 middle; 5: 249-254 top; 6: 254-270 middle; 7: 270-278 top; 8: 278-292 bottom.

[2] CR 40: 481.

[3] *Decades* V,6,253. 'Et verba Domini: Hoc est corpus meum, Hic est sanguis meus, non rigide ad literam exponenda sunt, quasi panis et vinum essentialiter seu corporaliter sint corpus et sanguis Christi: sed symbolice et sacramentaliter.' *Absoluta*, 19b.

[4] Sed adest piis animis per spiritus sui virtutem, quia non impedit Christi distantia, quominus suos mirabiliter pascat. ... Neque enim descendit ad nos Christus e coelo, neque oculis cernitur, sed fide tantum nobis adest.' CR 40: 481.

In several of its details, this line of response by Calvin seems to have influenced Bullinger's editing of the original when he prepared the *Decades*. But the main lines of persistent differences were emerging.

After a slight variation of emphasis over Bullinger's long dismissal of any consecrating words as a crude superstition, the dialogue resumed regarding the relationship of the sign and the signified. Bullinger insisted throughout on their distinction, opposing superstition and concluding that Christ's body is therefore not present in the sign of the bread. Calvin conceded the danger of superstition, but argued that this impoverished line of reasoning neglected God's truthfulness.

'There is a union complementary with the thing figured, lest the sign be empty, because that which the Lord represents in a sign he effects at the same time, and executes in us by the power of his Spirit.'[1]

Here Calvin introduces two themes which will reappear often in his dialogue with Bullinger: that the signs are not empty, and that what God represents God also effects at the same time (*simul*).

For Bullinger, 'the sign and the signified are coupled together by God's institution,'[2] and by symbolic language which can call bread, or a rock, Christ. Calvin suspected Zwingli's influence in this view of symbolic language and protested that the Spirit has been neglected in such examples as Caesar on a coin. 'For where is the Spirit in the image of Caesar? Who in any way vivifies it? How is it efficacious in our hearts?'[3]

Bullinger's treatise continues and concludes with chapters nine through sixteen, which were eventually revised into the seventh sermon of the fifth *Decade*. In this case, the title of *Decade* V, 7 is not merely a conflation and abbreviation of these chapter titles, but reflects several editorial omissions. The phrases in italics abbreviate the original chapter titles which were omitted altogether in the *Decades* sermon title; the chapter numbers are again added in brackets,

'[9] That we must reason reverently of sacraments, *their nature, virtue, and efficacy;* [10] that they do not give grace, neither have grace included in them. [11] *The sacraments do not offer [exhibit] that which they signify.* [12] Again, what the virtue and lawful end and use of sacraments is. [13] *The sacraments represent the things signified.* [14] *The sacraments unite the members of Christ in one body.* [15] That they profit not without faith; that they are not superfluous to the faithful; [16] And that they do not depend upon the worthiness or unworthiness of the minister.'[4]

The suppression of the titles to chapters thirteen and fourteen is of only minor interest, since the text itself of these chapters was not omitted and received only

---

[1] 'Unio est rei figuratae complementum: quo fit ne signum sit inane, quia Dominus quod signo repraesentat simul efficit, impletque in nobis spiritus sui virtute.' CR 40: 482.

[2] *Decades* V,6,279.

[3] CR 40: 482.

[4] *Decades* V,7,293. The chapters of the original correspond to the following pagination in Parker: 9: 294-301 top; 10: 301-316 middle; 11: none; 12: 316-327 middle; 13: 327-332 bottom; 14: 332-340 middle; 15: 340-348 bottom; 16: 349-351 end).

minor editing. But the omission of the title *and* the text of chapter eleven is of great interest since Calvin's heaviest and perhaps most persuasive criticism of Bullinger's original work came at exactly this point, continuing the discussion of chapter ten. Although the general outlines of these omissions and alterations can be pointed out, with their apparent significance, the precise editing which Bullinger performed on his treatise *Absoluta* or *de Sacramentis* in order to produce *Decades* V, 6 and 7 awaits a major study—perhaps a dissertation—which would collate and explicate the differences between these two versions of the same work. At least some of the changes can be traced to Calvin's influence, but an exhaustive analysis is beyond the scope of this study. Since Calvin's letter seems to refute some points not made in that 1551 publication, perhaps Bullinger also edited the 1545 manuscript somewhat before its 1551 publication by a Lasco, even though he later said that it was then published in its first form.

Bullinger's arguments that the sacraments neither confer nor offer grace dominate chapters ten and eleven of his book, and thus the opening sections of *Decades* V, 7. The sacraments cannot be 'instruments, implements, and conduits, of grace because grace must precede proper reception, lest the sacraments be seen, unevangelically, as our work.[1] For Bullinger, several basic points of the Reformation must be maintained. Contrary to the old view of the law, including its ceremonial requirements, our salvation is entirely God's gracious doing. Therefore, any hint that our celebrations contribute something to salvation implied works righteousness, and any attachment of God's grace to a material object was idolatrous. The sacraments do not confer grace, since they do not contain grace in themselves, to be crassly conveyed as if by channels or pipes. Such an exaltation of the material would be 'repugnant unto true religion,' since 'these things are spiritual, and therefore are brought to pass by the gift and mediation of the Holy Ghost.'[2] The sacraments, therefore, do not confer grace.

Calvin responded that the word 'confer' should not be understood so rigidly. Bullinger should not suspect works righteousness and idolatry everywhere. 'Is this the transfer of God's glory to creatures, when an instrument is used for distributing his grace? Then the sun does not illuminate the earth, nor bread nourish.'[3] Such a crude idolatry as Bullinger fears is a past error, not a present danger, for clearly the sacraments are not idols but aids or helps (*adiumenta, adminicula*).

But Calvin has saved his major arguments for Bullinger's eleventh chapter. 'The sacraments do not offer what they signify,' announced Bullinger's next chapter title.[4] Here too he is at pains to avoid idolatry and any restriction of God's free grace to material captivity and human manipulation. On the basis of the Scriptures and St. Augustine, Bullinger critiques Lombard, Aquinas, and Bonaventure. 'If the sacraments offer that which they signify, they certainly have

---

[1] *Ibid*, 294, 301f., 303, 305f.

[2] *Ibid*, 309-311.

[3] CR 40, 483.

[4] 'Sacramenta non exhibere quae significant,' *Absoluta* 68b.

or contain in themselves that which they offer. But what I do not have, I am not able to give to another.'[1]

Calvin expressed surprise and a sharp critique, even declaring that he would prefer the Thomist argument to the 'illusion' that Christ pointed to bread and wine, and promised his body and blood, but did not really mean it. The sacrament is 'nothing more than a channel so that it might be an implement of God.'[2] They do contain the grace of God, not crudely, but as Christ is contained in the gospel, and exhibited to us through the gospel. *Exhibeo* here concerns not a weak sense of a visual aid exhibit, but a strong statement that the sacraments 'truly offer' or 'give' what they signify, which Bullinger denied and Calvin affirmed. For Calvin, 'a sign is not set forth by God as empty.... It is God alone [not humans with their signs] who effects by his Spirit what he figures by the symbol.'[3] To Bullinger's worries that the sacraments as instruments detract from God, Calvin responded, 'what indeed do we abrogate or take away from God when we teach that he acts through his instruments, indeed he alone?'[4] True, agreed Calvin, some measure of grace and of Christ is present before receiving the sacrament; but there is growth in grace and in receiving Christ, precisely in the sacraments. Calvin countered Bullinger's every scriptural argument, and repeated often that the sacraments are indeed God's own instruments or implements, as are the ministers themselves.[5] Despite Bullinger's exertions, his sacraments end up empty, concluded Calvin.[6]

On the one hand, it may seem that Bullinger was persuaded by such argumentation, since this entire chapter was omitted when he converted his book into a part of the *Decades*. He deleted his explicit denial that the sacraments offer that which they signify. On the other hand, he did not abandon his major argument. If the choice is between empty sacraments or sacraments full in terms of containing grace in themselves, 'truly, I had rather confess them to be void than full.'[7] But they are not at all empty, in terms of God's true purpose for them. This is Bullinger's transition from what the sacraments are not to what they are:

> 'Therefore they that are partakers of the sacraments do not receive nothing, as these say, unless the institution of God be to be esteemed as nothing. He instituted sacraments to be testimonies of his grace, and seals of the truth of his promises.'[8]

---

[1] 'Caeterum si sacramenta quod significant exhibent, certe habent aut in se continent, quod exhibent. Quod enim non habeo, alteri dare non possum.' *Ibid.*

[2] '... quia nihil plus tribuo sacramento, quam ut sit Dei organum.' CR 40: 484.

[3] 'Signum enim a Deo vacuum non proficiscitur.... Solus est Deus qui efficit spiritu suo quod symbolo figurat.' *Ibid.* For Calvin on exhibeo, see Tylenda, 'Ecumenical Intention,' (note 2 on p.5 above), 31.

[4] 'Quid enim Deo abrogamus aut derogamus quum ipsum tradimus agere per sua instrumenta, et quidem solum?' *Ibid,* 485.

[5] *Ibid,* 485f. Besides the quotations above (notes 2 and 4 above), see CR 40: 486 for another use of *instrumenta* and 487f. for two uses of *organum*.

[6] *Ibid,* 488.

[7] *Decades* V,7, 314.

[8] *Ibid,* 315.

Bullinger's original chapter twelve pursued this main point, that the sacraments testify, seal, confirm and bear witness to the truth of God's promises in the gospel.[1] Zwingli is lightly invoked regarding the functions of official and divine seals, confirming the truth of the message. But the main thrust of the argument is in Bullinger's own understanding of the sacraments as testimonies, by analogy or similitude, as set out in chapter thirteen.

For Bullinger, the sacraments signify in that they testify or point out by means of signs. They do not bring or give grace, but resemble it.

'Now in the Lord's Supper bread and wine represent the very body and blood of Christ. The reason hereof is this. As bread nourisheth and strengtheneth man, and giveth him ability to labour; so the body of Christ, eaten by faith, feedeth and satisfieth the soul of man, and furnisheth the whole man to all duties of godliness. As wine is drink to the thirsty, and maketh merry the hearts of men; so the blood of our Lord Jesus, drunken by faith, doth quench the thirst of the burning conscience, and filleth the hearts of the faithful with unspeakable joy.'[2]

For Bullinger, it was crucial that the actions of our Lord's Supper carefully duplicate the actions of the Last Supper, for Christ chose these actions to be analogous to spiritual activities. He extends this analogy to *our* breaking the bread and pouring out the wine, 'for we ourselves are in fault that he was torn and tormented.'[3] Bullinger's use of analogy often employs this literary structure of comparison: 'as . . ., so . . .':

'Therefore, as the sustenance of bread and wine, passing into the bowels, is changed into the substance of man's body; even so Christ, being eaten of the godly by faith, is united unto them by his Spirit.[4]

After this discussion, explicitly entitled 'the analogy of the sign and the signified,' Bullinger's treatise moves quickly to a close, as accurately summarized in the chapter titles listed above.

As for Calvin's response, after his long critique of what Bullinger said that the sacrament is not (a conferring or offering of grace), he pays little attention to what Bullinger says the sacrament *is*, namely, a testimony to grace or an analogy of grace. He only remarks tersely: 'now this is the analogy, that as the soul is fed by the flesh of Christ, just so is the body by the bread.'[5]

After his thorough criticism, Calvin was concerned for Bullinger's reaction. Mindful of your request, he wrote (to paraphrase), I have skimmed over the commendable parts in order to note where it could be improved. I have fulfilled your wish and discharged the duty of a friend; now it is up to you to attribute my

---

[1] *Ibid,* 316-318, 324.

[2] *Ibid,* 329. Bullinger spoke of the analogy of baptism's water (cleansing, refreshing, and cooling) on pp. 328f., and *Decades* V, 8, 364.

[3] *Ibid.* 330. See also the *Warhaffte Bekanntnus* 75a, and *Decades* V, 9, 416-422.

[4] *Ibid.* See also the explicit references to analogy, and the use of the structure 'as . . ., so . . .' in *Decades* V, 6, 244 and 280, as well as in V, 9, 410 and 467.

[5] 'Atque haec analogia est, ut vescatur Christi carne anima, sicuti corpus pane.' CR 40: 488. Calvin also used the concept of analogy, especially in catechetical context: *Geneva Catechism* 51. 341.

freedom to good will and simple obedience.[1] Calvin was apparently right to be apprehensive about Bullinger's reaction to such a thorough and forthright critique, for the response from Zurich was a cool suspension of correspondence. Later that year (1547) Calvin wrote,

> It is now six months since I returned your book, with annotations, such as you had requested me to make. I am surprised that I have received no reply from you since that time.[2]

Calvin was increasingly concerned, not for abstract theological reasons, but because of the concrete political and military situation. In this same letter, he wrote about the calamity in Germany, where the Emperor's Counter-Reformation armies were enjoying considerable success. Calvin pressed Bullinger to see the urgency of the situation.

> 'Were he to enter Strasbourg, he would, you perceive, occupy an encampment whence he could invade us. Would there then be time, my Bullinger, for you to deliberate? For by keeping silence, do you not, as it were, present your throat to be cut?'[3]

In the sixteenth century a military alliance often depended upon an explicit confessional agreement. In this case, Calvin knew that the Swiss Protestant cities would never form an effective military confederation without an open doctrinal consensus, which met its greatest barrier at precisely this point, the Lord's Supper.

Bullinger apparently responded by the end of that year in a letter considered by Calvin's editors and others to be lost, although the current exhaustive editing of Bullinger's works may prove otherwise. In any case, Calvin commented sharply on this subject to his colleague Viret in a letter dated 23 January 1548:

> 'Here you also have [as enclosed?] the letter of Bullinger, in which you will see an amazing *authadeian* [Greek for audaciousness]. I once commented to you about the Zurichers, that they always sing the same song. If only stubbornness did not always please them, under the pretext of perseverance. Now you understand that you were wrong when you thought that something was accomplished in my letter, to which he responds in this way, as if I had challenged him to combat in the arena.'[4]

Although Bullinger much later remembered Calvin's response to his book as not disapproval but praise[5], these comments by Calvin about Bullinger's tardy and touchy response indicate that the Zuricher did not appreciate the Genevan's critique.

---

[1] CR 40: 489.

[2] 13 October 1547, CR 40: 590; Bonnet II, p. 143 (here dated 19 September 1547).

[3] *Ibid.* 590f.; Bonnet II, p. 144.

[4] 'Habes hic etiam literas Bullingeri, in quibus videbis miram authadeian [in Greek]. Dixi tibi de Tigurinis aliquando, eos semper unum canere. Utinam non usque adeo illis constantiae praetextu arrideret contumacia. Nunc te fuisse deceptum intelliges qui putabas aliquid me profecturum ea epistola cui sic respondet ac si fuisset a me in arenam provocatus.' CR 40: 654.

[5] 'Anno salutis 1546 scripsi librum De Sacramentis, quem primo quidem misi ad D. Caluinum, qui non improbauit, sed laudauit.' Staedtke bibliography, 91.

At this point, in early 1548, the outlook for agreement must have seemed bleak, although Bullinger's letter could shed different light on the situation. A genuine difference in sacramental theology had been acknowledged on both sides. Calvin considered the Lord's Supper to be an instrument of God's grace, whereby believers commune in the body and blood of Christ. Bullinger explicitly rejected such 'instrumentalism' and considered the Supper to be a testimony to or an analogy of God's grace, whereby God testified to the believers, through the analogy of bread and wine nourishing and invigorating our bodies, concerning the salvation and nourishment won in Christ's body and blood, received in faith. The contrast between the sacrament as an instrument or as a testimony was a substantial difference, fully acknowledged on both sides. To summarize it baldly, Calvin proposed and Bullinger opposed the language of instrument (*instrumentum*) and implement (*organum*). In fact, the Zurich ministers had called such instrumentalism 'Thomist and scholastic' in a statement to the Bern clergy.[1] Calvin, on the other hand, had said in his response to Bullinger's book that he would prefer Thomism to illusory, empty signs, and had written in his *Response* to the Council of Trent, that he agreed with its condemnation of those who say that the sacraments do not contain the grace they figure.[2] Thomism and Trent aside, there seemed to be an impasse, a stalemate between Geneva and Zurich, not to mention the Germans and the other Swiss cities.

---

[1] 'Ministri dicuntur instrumenta per quae Deus fidem conferat. Sacramenta dicuntur instrumenta per quae infunditur gratia. Imo per ministros et sacramenta perficiuntur fideles. Id quod Thomisticum et scholasticum esse nostis. Ministri et sacramenta nihil conferunt, sed annunciant. Deus confert omnia.' 17 January 1547, CR 40: 471f. The Zurichers' objections to the implications of *per* and *instrumenta* became the major point of disagreement with Calvin, discussed below.

[2] CR 40: 454, discussed in context above (note 2 on p.25), and (regarding Trent) CR 35: 494, 'Antidote to the Council of Trent,' *Tracts and Treatises* III, 174. Bullinger's suspicions of Calvin's affinities with 'Scholastics, Papists, and Sophists' were to become explicit as their correspondence continued, specifically over the first of the 'Twenty-four propositions' (CR 35: 693). See Gerrish's comments about 'Thomistic' and 'Franciscan' strains in the Reformed tradition, 'Sign and Reality: The Lord's Supper in the Reformed Confessions,' *The Old Protestantism and the New*, 128f. This chapter is based on an article in *Theology Today* 23 (1966): 224-243. See also Gäbler, TRE 8, 189f. Although Bullinger himself was quick to critique Scholasticism, he also 'learned much from the Schoolmen.' Hughes Oliphant Old, 'Bullinger and the Scholastic Works on Baptism; A Study in the History of Christian Worship,' *Heinrich Bullinger 1504-1575* I, 91-207 (see note 1 on p.12).

# Part II. The Agreement

Despite Calvin's obvious disappointment with Bullinger's reaction to his critique, as expressed in the letter to Viret, the Genevan pursued diplomacy, not polemics. On 1 March, 1548 he wrote a brief and conciliatory letter to Bullinger:

'I pass over in silence the long reply in which you seek to wash away all those points of difference about which I had carefully admonished you. or of what avail is it for us to enter on a controversy? ... I responded at your request. ... But in whatever way I may affirm a greater communication of Christ in the Sacraments than you express in words, let us not on that account, cease to hold the same Christ, and to be one in him. Someday, perhaps, it will be given us to unite in fuller harmony of opinion.'[1]

Calvin wished to persuade Bullinger of his sincerity in pursuing such a harmony, yet without equivocating on his basic position. No matter what rumours Bullinger may have heard to the contrary, 'I used the same language at Zurich as at Geneva.'[2] He again reminded his correspondent of the sad news on the military confessional front, this time from France.

Bullinger responded to this brief conciliatory overture with a similar tone in his letter of 26 May 1548:

'understand what your judgment is regarding my response. Thus I too will cease repeating what has been expounded before. Meanwhile, with God who knows the heart as my witness, I am not able to think differently than I think, nor to speak differently than I have spoken. I acknowledge that Christ communicates himself totally to us in his Spirit, by faith, insofar as this is necessary for our salvation, and for us to live faithfully. This is what is signified to us in the sacraments and is sealed in a manner appropriate to sacraments, just as it is also announced in the word, and, by being testified, is inculcated.'[3]

Here Bullinger is equally conciliatory in manner, but just as forthright about his basic position, namely, that the sacrament is not God's instrument or means of grace, but God's testimony to grace. While the centres of their positions have not

---

[1] 'Longam illam responsionem, in qua omnia de quibus te admonueram accurate diluere conaris, silentio praetereo. Quid enim attinet inter nos disceptare? ... Feceram id tuo rogatu. ... Verum utcunque maior Christi communicatio mihi in sacramentis constet, quam verbis tuis exprimas, non tamen proptera desinemus eundem habere Christum et in ipso unum esse. Aliquando forte in consensum pleniorem coalescere dabitur'. CR 40: 666; Bonnet II, 160.

[2] *Ibid.*

[3] 'Agnosco Christum in spiritu suo per fidem se totum nobis communicare, quantum nobis ad salutem consequendam et ad pie vivendum necessarium est. Id quod sacramentis nobis significatur et obsignatur more sacramentis proprio quemadmodum et verbo annunciatur testificandoque inculcatur.' CR 40: 706.

changed, both Calvin and Bullinger seem more open to each other and to a process of shared dialogue in search of agreement. The reasons for this apparent thaw in their correspondence are several, and may relate to Calvin's visit to Zurich in the spring of 1548, a visit without substantive dialogue on these points.[1] But the presenting cause for this openness was probably the sudden sense of urgency over the military threat of the Counter-Reformation, as exemplified by the Augsburg Interim in Germany.

As the provisional basis of a religious settlement between Roman Catholics and Lutherans, the text of the Augsburg Interim was privately circulated during the spring of 1548, before its formal adoption in late June of that year. Like Calvin, Bullinger had a definite reaction to it. His 26 May letter continues: 'This Interim is nothing but papism itself. . . . I have also seen Melanchthon's counsel. Good God, what panic and dislocation! . . . The Interim article on the sacraments, principally on the eucharist, is completely papist.'[2]

Calvin welcomed Bullinger's new cooperative spirit, and shared his concern for the overall political-confessional-military situation. His response of 6 July concludes, 'But may the very fewness of our numbers incite us to an alliance!'[3] This letter seized the opportunity to propose a statement on the Lord's Supper, in the spirit of direct negotiations based on good faith in spite of acknowledged differences. Calvin began by lamenting the absence of personal, face-to-face discussions on the topic, especially since he had been in Zurich recently. He continued with a detailed statement on the sacraments, especially the Lord's Supper.

But before Bullinger actually received this letter, he wrote Calvin again, on 14 July. By this time the Augburg Interim was officially adopted, which prompted Bullinger to condemn it even more bitterly, and to ask Calvin to send him some pertinent literature. He concludes, 'The Lord will have pity on his most afflicted church.'[4] Calvin's letter did not arrive until August, and Bullinger did not respond until October. Just at this time the Roman Catholic Imperial forces occupied Constance, a strategic point on the Swiss-German border near Zurich. Bullinger's October letter to Calvin expressed his deep alarm in penitent, apocalyptic terms.[5]

Nevertheless, in November of that year, Bullinger responded carefully to Calvin's June letter and its statement about the sacraments, which he put into a series of twenty-four propositions and critiqued one by one, not rushing into any doctrinal compromise even if the need for an alliance was dire. This detailed commentary (called 'Annotations') was answered, point by point, in Calvin's 'Response' in January 1549. Then Bullinger made his final comments (entitled

---

[1] CR 40: 727. Did Bullinger refuse to discuss it? CR 40: 720.

[2] CR 40: 707.

[3] CR 40: 730; Bonnet II, 172, dating it 26 June.

[4] CR 41: 7.

[5] 'Meremur ut nos flagello excitet Dominus. Hic tamen clemens est et propitius. . . . Si placet ei nos ex hoc eripere saeculo, innumeris liberarit malis, vita donabit eterna.' 15 October 1548, CR 41: 60f.

'Notes') in March 1549. Thus Calvin's original letter and the three subsequent pamphlets (Bullinger's Annotations, Calvin's Response, and Bullinger's Notes, each about seven columns of text) can be treated together, point and counterpoint.[1] With their accompanying correspondence, these writings constitute the two Reformers' fullest direct negotiations over the Lord's Supper, and reveal their positions quite thoroughly.

Although lengthy, Calvin's letter should first be quoted in full, with Bullinger's editing into propositions indicated by the added italics and the numbers in brackets.

For with regard to the Sacraments in general, [1] *we neither bind up the grace of God with them,* [2] *nor transfer to them the work of power of the Holy Spirit,* [3] *nor do we locate in them the assurance of salvation.* We expressly declare that [4] *it is God alone who acts by means of the Sacraments; and we maintain that their whole efficacy is due to the Holy Spirit,* and testify that [5] *this action appears only in the elect.* [6] *Nor do we teach that the sacrament is of profit, otherwise than as it leads us by the hand to Christ, that we may seek in him whatever blessings there are.* I do not in truth see what you can properly desire as wanting in this doctrine, which teaches that salvation is to be sought from Christ alone, makes God its sole author, and asserts that it is accepted only through the secret working of the Spirit. We teach, however, that [7] *the sacraments are instruments of the grace of God;* for, as they were instituted in view of a certain end, we refuse to allow that they have no proper use. We therefore say, that *what is represented in them, is offered to the elect, for [8] God does not delude the eyes by a fallacious representation.* [9] *Thus we say, that he who receives baptism* with true faith, *further receives by it [at the same time] the remission of sins.* But lest any one should ascribe his salvation to baptism as the cause, we at the same time subjoin the explanation, that [10] *the remission flows from the blood of Christ,* and that [11] *it is accordingly conferred by baptism only in so far as this is a testimony of the cleansing which the Son of God by his own blood shed on the cross procured for us, and which he offers for our enjoyment by faith in his gospel, and brings to perfection in our hearts by his Spirit.* Our opinion regarding regeneration is precisely similar to that about baptism.

[12] *When the signs of the flesh and blood of Christ are spread before us in the Supper, we say that they are not spread before us in vain, but that the thing itself is also manifested to us.* [13] *Whence it follows, that we eat the body and drink the blood of Christ.* By so speaking, [14] *we neither make the sign the thing, nor confound both in one,* [15] *nor enclose the body of Christ in the bread,* nor, on the other hand, imagine it to be infinite, [16] *nor dream of a carnal transfusion of Christ into us,* nor lay down any other fiction of that sort. You maintain that [17] *Christ, as to his human nature, is in heaven;* we also profess the same doctrine. [18] *The word 'heaven' implies,* in your view, *distance of place; we also readily adopt the opinion, that Christ is undoubtedly distant from us by an interval*

---

[1] *Oiannis Calvini Propositiones de Sacramentis. Annotationes breves adscripsit Henricus Bullingerus,* CR 35: 693-700; *Calvini Responsio ad ANNOTATIONES BULLINGERI. SCRIPTA MENSE IANUARIO 1549,* CR 35: 701-708; *HENRICI BULLINGERI ANNOTATA AD CALVINI ANIMADVERSIONES,* CR 35: 709-716.

*of place.* [19] *You deny that the body of Christ is infinite, but hold that it is contained within its circumference;* we candidly give an unhesitating assent to that view, and raise a public testimony on behalf of it. You refuse to allow the sign to be confounded with the thing; [14b] *we are sedulous in admonishing that the one should be distinguished from the other.* [15b] *You strongly condemn impanation;* we subscribe to your decision.

What then is the sum of our doctrine? [20] *It is this, that when we discern here on earth the bread and wine, our minds must be raised to heaven in order to enjoy Christ, and* [21] *that Christ is there present with us, while we seek him above the elements of this world.* [22] *For it is not permitted us to charge Christ with fallacy;* and that would be the case, unless we held that the reality is exhibited together with the sign. [23] *And you also concede that the sign is by no means empty.* [24] *It only remains that we define what it contains within it.* When we *briefly reply, that we are made partakers of the flesh and blood of Christ that he may dwell in us and we in him, and in this way enjoy all his benefits,* what is there, I ask, in these words either absurd or obscure, especially as we, in express terms, exclude whatever delirious fancies might occur to the mind?

Calvin goes on to defend his friend Bucer from Bullinger's criticism, including the latter's instructions to young Zurichers visiting Strasbourg not to commune in Bucer's church.[1]

As to the form and style of their negotiations, Calvin's letter reveals his conciliatory purpose in its opening sequence of negations. Mindful of their impasse over whether the sacraments confer grace or simply testify to it, he sought to reassure Bullinger that he did not bind grace too closely to the sacraments, as medieval superstitions seemed to suggest. Thus the first six 'propositions' (as well as nos. 10, 14-16, and 19), as Bullinger identified and numbered them, are negations designed to allay any such suspicions. Bullinger, however, was not appeased. Regarding the very first item, he wrote: 'I do not see how your teaching here differs from that of the papists, who teach that the sacraments themselves confer grace on all recipients.'[2] Calvin then explained that in his view grace is not bound to the sacraments but is connected to them; they are God's means of conferring grace, not to all, as the papists imply, but only to the elect.[3]

---

[1] CR 40: 727f.; the translation is altered only slightly from Bonnet II, 169f. Calvin later reminded Bullinger that he had accepted the latter's editing of his letter into a list of propositions (CR 35: 705 no. 11). Yet Bullinger's mistaken placement of the word *simul* in proposition 9, as bracketed in the above quotation, proved significant, as discussed below. For a guide to the correspondence between Bullinger and Bucer, and thus to their disagreements, see Jean Rott, 'Die Üerlieferung des Briefwechsels von Bullinger und den Zürchern mit Martin Bucer und den Strassburgern,' *Heinrich Bullinger 1504-1575* II, 257-286.

[2] 'Hic non video quid doctrina vestra discrepet a doctrina papistarum, qui docent sacramenta conferre gratiam omnibus sumentibus ipsa.' CR 35: 693 (no. 1). Yet Bullinger did not retreat from his charges regarding Scholastics or Sophists on proposition 9, CR 35: 695f. and 713.

[3] CR 35: 701 (no. 1).

While Bullinger later withdrew this particular accusation of papism, this exchange over the first proposition previews the tone and the substance of their overall negotiations. Bullinger's suspicions are explicit in his remarks on propositions 1-2, 4, 7, 9-11, 13, and 18-24. Calvin patiently explained himself again and again, but also let his exasperation show on occasion. To Bullinger's objections to proposition 13 on eating and drinking the body and blood of Christ, he marvels, 'you treat me as if you were negotiating with the crassest papist!'[1] More specifically, Calvin needed to disentangle himself from the Zurich (and Bern) suspicions that he was too close to the Lutherans on this issue. When Bullinger repeatedly insisted upon a finite body of Christ located in a distant heaven, Calvin exclaims,

> 'As if I indeed ought to bear the guilt, if the Lutherans sin! . . . As if on this point I might have something in common with them.[1]

When Calvin sent Bullinger the Response containing these comments, his cover letter summarized this question of a suspicious tone, an 'unprofitable distrust,' and asked Bullinger not to 'allow yourself to become entangled in baseless suspicions. . . . If there be any who have flattered Luther and others, I am not of that number.'[3] Bullinger's Notes of March 1549 indicated his appeasement, 'I know full well that you have nothing at all in common with them.'[4] In his cover letter, Bullinger apologized for warily insisting on explicit clarifications of so many points, and pronounced himself satisfied with most of them: 'that which I was hoping to hear from you in clear words, I have heard.'[5]

The more substantial side of their negotiations was also previewed in this initial exchange over the relationship of the sacraments and grace. In his Response, Calvin explicitly called the sacraments the 'means' (*media*) God uses,[6] although he did not here employ the expression 'means of grace.' Consistent with their previous correspondence, Bullinger preferred to call the sacraments 'testimonies of the grace of God.'[7] As to the relationship of the sacrament to the Holy Spirit (proposition 2), for Calvin the Spirit's proper work of making us partakers of Christ is done *per sacramenta*, 'through the sacraments, as through instruments. . . . the Spirit is the author, the sacrament is the instrument used.'[8] Indeed, proposition 4 explicitly stated that God works through the sacraments, which drew this comment from Bullinger:

> 'For this word "through" (*per*) seems to ascribe more to inanimate things, to

---

[1] CR 35: 705 (no. 13).

[2] 'Quasi vero, si quid Lutherani peccant, ego crimen sustinere debeam. Quasi aliquid in hac parte commune cum illis habeam. CR 35: 706 (no. 19).

[3] 21 January 1549, CR 41: 165; Bonnet II, 210.

[4] 'Ac ut clare intelligerem, te nihil prorsus com illis habere commune . . .' CR 35: 715 (no. 19).

[5] '. . . sed quod disertis verbis id a te audire cupiverim quod audivi.' 15 March 1549, CR 41: 221.

[6] CR 35: 701 (no. 1).

[7] CR 35: 709 (no. 1).

[8] 'Spiritus autor est, sacramentum vero instrumentum quo utitur.' CR 35: 702 (no. 2).

the signs of water, bread, and wine, than should be ascribed. The efficacy of any blessing should be rightly ascribed to the Holy Spirit.[1]

This objection prompted Calvin to a biblical review of how God works through baptism, through the laying on of hands, through the human voice, and through the ministry generally. None of this was persuasive to Bullinger, who viewed all these as external symbols and testimonies.[2] Even their agreement that the sacraments lead us to Christ (no. 6) uncovered the same fundamental difference. For Bullinger, the sacramental 'signs testify to and signify the celestial gifts'; for Calvin, they are the Spirit's very instruments.[3]

Their disagreement came to a head regarding proposition 7: 'The sacraments are instruments of the grace of God. For what is figured in them, we say is offered to the elect.'[4] Although Calvin here (and in proposition 5) seems to concede something new—that the objective grace of the sacraments is qualified by limiting their efficacy to the elect—Bullinger seems not to notice any progress here toward a Zurich 'subjectivism' and in fact expresses sharp disagreement on the heart of the matter:

> 'This proposition contains something which afflicts and irritates the faithful. If by 'instrument' you mean 'sign,' fine. But if it is something more than sign, you seem to ascribe too much to the sacraments. . . . It is God who saves and receives us in grace. But this you ascribe to an instrument through which it is worked, some implement or flow-sluice or canal, the very sacraments, through which grace is infused into us. . . . But we do not believe this. . . . God alone works our salvation. . . . God, and no created thing, confers and indeed confers through the Spirit and faith. . . . The sacraments neither offer nor confer, nor are they instruments of offering and conferring, but they signify, testify, and seal.'[5]

---

[1] 'Nam vocabulum Per videtur rebus inanimatis, aquae, pani et vino, signis inquam, plus tribuere quam tribuendum est. Recte quidem tribuitur omnis boni efficacia spiritui sancto.' CR 35: 694 (no. 4).

[2] CR 35: 702f. and 711 (both regarding no. 4).

[3] Bullinger: CR 35: 694 (no. 6); Calvin: CR 35: 703 (no. 6). In Bullinger's counterpoint note, he repeats that the sacraments 'signify, represent, seal, and attest' CR 35: 712 (no. 6).

[4] 'In Calvin's original letter: 'Atqui docemus, sacramenta gratiae Dei esse instrumenta. . . . Quod ergo illic figuratur dicimus electis exhiberi.' CR 40: 727f. In Bullinger's formulation: VII. 'Sacramenta sunt instrumenta gratiae Dei. Nam quod illis figuratur, dicimus exhiberi electis.' CR 35: 695.

[5] 'Haec propositio habet quod pios affligat et urat. Si per instrumentum intelligis signum, bene est. Si amplius quiddam quam signum, videris sacramentis nimium tribuere. . . . Deus is est qui nos salvat et recipit in gratiam. Huic vos tribuitis instrumentum per quod operetur, organum inquam, et infundibulum, ac canalem quendam, ipsa inquam sacramenta, per quae nobis infundat gratiam. . . . Caeterum nos non ita credimus, . . . Deus solus operatur salutem nostram . . . Deus, nulla creatura, conferat, et conferat quidem per spiritum et fidem. . . . Sacramenta illa non exhibent aut conferunt, ceu exhibendi et conferendi instrumenta, sed significant, testificantur et obsignant'. CR 35: 695 (no. 7). Bullinger also says here that the signs, being inanimate, are not capable (capacia) of spiritual things, which receives Calvin's agreement: 'Quod obiicis, non esse donorum Dei capax signum visibile, quum res sit inanima, id ego tecum fateor.' CR 35: 703 (no. 7).

Bullinger consistently insisted that all the credit go, evangelically, to God, whose Spirit works on the soul directly, without crass intermediaries like implements or canals for grace, which he viewed as a medieval superstition. Here he explicitly rejects the terminology of instrument and implement (*organum*).

Calvin responded that of course everything is ascribed to God, 'but what is your argument, that God alone acts, therefore all instruments cease?'[1] What is figured in the sacrament is also offered therein, not because the sacraments are crude channels inclosing material grace, but because they are God's instruments for conferring grace, as the human voice is an instrument of God's saving work. Calvin reminded Bullinger of their previous disagreement: 'what you deny to be conferred through the sacraments, I affirm.'[2] Bullinger's rebuttal conceded nothing. Even praising gifted people such as Calvin himself is actually to praise God; certainly inanimate creations should not divert us from praising the Creator. 'God alone does it, and what God does, implements (*organa*) do not do.' The sacramental 'instruments,' if Calvin insists on this term, do only what they were instituted to do, namely, represent and seal the gifts of God, 'just as the preacher's voice only announces what God perfects in the soul through the Spirit.'[3]

On one point, regarding proposition nine, Calvin and Bullinger found themselves entangled in a curious debate apparently based upon the mistaken placement of the word *[simul.]* According to the printed edition, Calvin had written whoever 'receives baptism in true faith receives by it the remission of sins.' Mindful of Bullinger's concerns not to bind grace to the rites, he hastened to add, 'but at the same time *simul* we subjoin this explanation, lest any one ascribe his salvation to baptism, that the remission flows from the blood of Christ.'[4] Calvin's caution backfired on him as Bullinger mistakenly read the word *simul* one line too soon, yielding 'whoever receives baptism, at the same time *[simul]* receives the remission of sins.' In this mistaken word order, the particle *simul* offended Bullinger, since Abraham was justified before circumcision, and it bound grace too closely to the sacraments, as the Scholastics taught.[5]

At this point, one might expect Calvin's response to clear up the question of word order, and/or to address the substance of the issue and defend such an understanding of *simul.* Calvin's entire concept of the sacraments as God's instruments of grace did involve a simultaneity of sacrament and grace, in this case a simultaneity of baptism and forgiveness, while yet not confining grace to the sacraments. But Calvin did not disavow this word order and point out his original text, now nine months old, nor did he vigorously defend the simultaneity implicit in his understanding of the sacraments as instruments.

---

[1] 'Vide tamen quale sit tuum argumentum: Deus solus agit; cessant igitur instrumenta.' Quid? CR 35: 703 (no. 7).

[2] 'Quin potius, et iam ante tibi memini me scripsisse, inde, quod tu improbas, colligo, per sacramenta quoque conferri.' CR 35: 704 (no. 7).

[3] 'Deus agit solus, ergo id quod Deus agit non agunt organa. . . . sacramenta dona Dei repraesentant et obsignant.' CR 35: 712 (no. 7).

[4] CR 40: 728 (see note 1 on p.32 above).

[5] CR 35: 695f.

Instead, he reassured Bullinger that he never meant *simul* to denote a temporal restriction of grace. Instead, it meant *similiter* (similarly) in this sense: 'that we truly become participants in the thing signified, even as we discern the sign with our eyes.'[1] This, Calvin concluded, the Sophists would never approve. Bullinger responded that he did not oppose this meaning of *simul* as *similiter*, but that it would be simpler and safer to say that whoever receives baptism receives a symbol or seal of forgiveness. He did not relent regarding the Scholastics or Sophists, noting that these theologians found less to oppose in the Lutherans or in Calvin than in the Zurichers.[2]

This exchange is significant on both sides. For Bullinger, his explicit rejection of the sacraments as *simultaneous* testimonies must be compared with his qualification on this point much later in the *Second Helvetic Confession*, to be mentioned below. For Calvin, his explicit concession on this point was probably not a genuine change in his thinking, since he was consistent on this issue everywhere else, maintaining at least a discreet silence on it with Bullinger. Rather, it seems that Calvin here continued his overall approach of accommodating his terminology as much as possible, even risking occasional distortion, in order to reassure Bullinger and to secure an agreement.

Nevertheless, a fundamental point of difference remained. Of the twenty-four propositions, only two did not receive eventual agreement within this exchange of mini-treatises, yet these two revealed the foundational difference between Calvin and Bullinger: the fourth proposition, on God acting through (*per*) the sacraments, and the seventh, on the sacraments as instruments of grace. Furthermore, in several other cases, the propositions precipitated interpretive comments which revealed the same underlying conflict over Calvin's 'instrumentalism.' On the other hand, when Calvin's text spoke more modestly about the sacraments as testimonies, as in the eleventh proposition, Bullinger was enthusiastic. 'In these lines shines a great hope of agreement. ... The entire business can be condensed under this heading.'[3] Calvin's concluding comments (on proposition 24) seemed to cultivate this positive reaction in his correspondent. Instead of reinforcing what had originally been his letter's strong conclusion about partaking of Christ's flesh and blood, he seems rather to accommodate his language to Bullinger's by denying any crude notion of inclosure in the bread and wine. He further quoted from the Genevan liturgy on the bread and wine as 'sign and testimonies,' which we do not cling to, since we 'lift up our minds where Christ dwells in the glory of the Father.'[4] Surely Calvin knew that Bullinger would find these words from Geneva more to his liking than Calvin's further claims for the sacraments as instruments. Indeed, Bullinger's own conclusion repeated these liturgical quotations, and added 'This I approve, to these comments I subscribe.'[5] In summary, when Calvin spoke of the sacraments as testimonies to grace rather than as instruments of grace, agreement

---

[1] CR 35: 704.
[2] CR 35: 713.
[3] CR 35: 696 (no. 11).
[4] CR 35: 708 (no. 24).
[5] CR 35: 716 (no. 24).

flourished, for this was Bullinger's theme throughout this exchange and indeed throughout his entire corpus.[1]

Bullinger's cover letter of 15 March 1549 (sent with his final commentary or Notes) immediately emphasized the positive:

'O learned Calvin, most dear brother, you certainly progressed a lot with me by your response.... I hope that when you have read my response, all dissension on this matter will be settled.... Hereafter let complaints depart. Let us love each other with a mutual sincerity, and let us build up the churches.'[2]

For the moment, Zurich was under less immediate military threat than the previous Autumn and Bullinger wanted to keep it that way. The situation in Germany looked worse and worse, as most of the churches accepted the Interim. 'Let us pray for them, I beseech you, and may all of us here in Switzerland consult so that our churches may be in concord.'[3] In this cover letter, Bullinger's explicit expressions of mutual love and of the need for an agreement indicated his rapidly increasing openness to consummate the negotiations with Calvin.

At this point, Bullinger and Calvin had achieved considerable agreement and had received reassurances about each other's positions. The political need for an explicit alliance was clearly pressing, and their remaining doctrinal differences were now identified with sufficient precision as to isolate their options. Either Calvin would refrain from speaking of God as working through (*per*) the sacraments, and of the sacraments as God's instruments or implements of grace, or else Bullinger would change his position and openly agree that the sacraments were not only testimonies, analogies, and parallels to grace, but God's very instruments for conferring grace. The next six months saw a sudden turn of events, but at least the detailed correspondence before May of 1549 clarifies the underlying issue in sacramental theology and terminology between Calvin and Bullinger and thus the context for assessing what happened during the rest of that year.

### THE ZURICH CONSENSUS (CONSENSUS TIGURINUS)

From here on, the narrative concerns material directly associated with the *Consensus Tigurinus* of 1549 (the 'Zurich Consensus'), and thus fairly well known, at least to diligent students of the Reformation. Less familiar, even to specialists,

---

[1] In his original Annotations, Bullinger sounded this theme, of the sacraments as testimonies, regarding propositions 4-8, 11, 17, 23, and 24. In his final Notes, he repeated it regarding 1-2, 4-6, 12, and 24.

[2] 'Multum sane profecisti apud me tua responsione, Calvine octissime et carissime frater. ... Lecta responsione mea spero te hac in causa omnem positurum dissensionem. Valeant porro expostulationes. Amemus nos mutuo sincere et aedificemus ecclesias.' CR 41: 221.

[3] 'Oremus pro illis, obsecro, et huc conferamus vires omnes in Helvetia ut ecclesiae nostrae sint concordes. *Ibid,* 223.

are the detailed, private negotiations between Calvin and Bullinger discussed above. Yet only they can provide the necessary context for appreciating the nuances of this public document and its influence on Reformed theologians and their confessional writings.

Bullinger's letter of 15 March and his final Notes on the twenty-four propositions received no answer from Calvin until 7 May. Such mail had been especially gratifying, Calvin then wrote, since he needed some good news during the sad period of mourning over the death of his wife. Indeed, it may be that he had received this correspondence near the first of April, quite close to his wife's death, but could not return to work until May out of grief, as poignantly evident in his letters to Viret and Farel. In any case, Calvin's letter of May 7 shared Bullinger's warm hope for agreement, and also his sense of urgency. 'For I am very glad that hardly anything—or at least very little—hinders us from agreeing now even in words.'[1] Most of the letter concerned Calvin's Old Testament arguments in favor of concluding an alliance with the new King of France, even if spiritually compromising, since the overall calamities were so dire and threatened the very ruin of the church.[2] He suggested coming to Zurich for a direct, face-to-face meeting.

Bullinger responded immediately (May 11), tenderly consoling Calvin in his grief, and discouraging him from abandoning his parish for such a costly and exhausting trip. Still favouring correspondence to direct meetings, Bullinger extolled the value of continuing their exchange of letters.[3] Nevertheless, it seems that before Calvin received this letter urging him not to come he had in fact already left Geneva for Zurich. Entirely consistent with their overall relationship, the initiative for personal dialogue came from Calvin. He stopped first in Neuchatel to be joined by Farel, who had urged him to overcome his grief and seize the moment for an agreement with Zurich. The meeting itself was in late May, after the 25th; but many details such as the exact date remain uncertain. Some hints surfaced later in related correspondence, such as Calvin's remarks that the trip was arranged in an abrupt two days, and that the entire issue was settled in a single session lasting only two hours.[4] As to the actual progress of the meeting, the historical record has left nothing like the Marburg narratives. Hardly anything about the session can be reconstructed. Calvin later wrote Bucer that things seemed hopeless at first, but 'suddenly light broke out.'[5] Yet some of

---

[1] 'Plurimum enim gaudeo nihil fere, aut quam minimum, restare, quin verbis etiam inter nos consentiamus'. CR 41: 266. Bonnet II, 225.

[2] CR 41: 267-269; Bonnet II, 226-228. The motive of persuading Zurich to join the alliance with France is also evident in the Geneva *Annales* for 20 May 1549 (CR 49: 452).

[3] CR 41: 278-280. Bullinger also held fast to the Zurich objection against any compromising alliance with France over against the emperor, even if it meant military disaster.

[4] Calvin to Oswald Myconius, 6 December 1549, CR 41: 456f. However, the diplomatic point of this letter was to reassure Myconius that the trip had developed so quickly and successfully that there was no time to include others, such as Myconius. Calvin here gave Farel major credit for the success of the trip. Bouvier, 140f.

[5] 'Subita lux affulsit.' CR 41: 440; Bonnet II, 235f.

these comments after the fact were also meant to portray the meeting in a positive light as genuinely smooth and successful. Actually, Calvin also later revealed that some Zurichers were reluctant to agree, whereas Bullinger much later remembered that Calvin tried to promote some terminology which was suspiciously 'Bucerian'.[1]

After some negotiations during the summer over the final editing, the text was ready by September of 1549. Rather quickly, considering the previous pattern of long and slow negotiations, a Geneva-Zurich consensus was finalized and shared with other Swiss cities and interested individuals.

The full text of the *Consensus,* only a handful of pages, is easily available in English translation. Although portions will be quoted below in the course of this presentation, an overview is gained through the list of paragraph headings. The original title, first of all, was 'Mutual Consensus in the Sacramental Issue by the Ministers of the Zurich Church and D. John Calvin Minister of the Geneva Church.' The phrase 'Consensus Tigurinus' or 'Zurich Consensus' dates from the nineteenth century.[2]

Mutual Consensus
 1. The entire spiritual regimen of the church leads us to Christ.
 2. The true knowledge of the sacraments from the knowledge of Christ.
 3. What the knowledge of Christ [is].
 4. Christ as priest. Christ as king.
 5. How Christ communicates himself to us.
 6. Spiritual communication. The sacraments instituted.
 7. The ends of the sacraments.
 8. What the sacraments truly figure, the Lord truly presents; thanksgiving.
 9. The signs and the things signified are distinct.
10. It is chiefly the promise which should be regarded in the sacraments.
11. One should not be awed at the elements.
12. By themselves the sacraments effect nothing.
13. God uses the implement, but such that all the virtue is God's.
14. [No title; quoted in full below].
15. How the sacraments strengthen.
16. Not all participants in the sacrament participate in the thing itself.
17. The sacraments do not confer grace.
18. God's gifts are offered to all, but only the faithful perceive them.
19. The faithful communicate in Christ before and apart from the use of the sacraments.
20. Grace is not bound to the action of the sacraments; their fruit is sometimes perceived after the action.

---

[1] Calvin to Bucer, CR 41: 439, Bonnet II, 235; Calvin to Sulzer, CR 41: 458; Bullinger to Beza, Bouvier, 562.

[2] Consensio Mutua in re Sacramentaria Ministrorum Tigurinae Ecclesiae et D. Ioannis Calvini Ministri Genevensis Ecclesiae.' Details of the origins of the title 'Consensus Tigurinus' are provided in the article by Gäbler, *TRE* 8: 189.

21. The notion of a local [presence] should be rejected.
22. An exposition of the words of the Lord's Supper, 'This is my body.'
23. On the eating of Christ's flesh.
24. Against transubstantiation and other follies.
25. The body of Christ is in heaven as in a place.
26. Christ should not be adored in the bread or the sacrament.[1]

It is immediately apparent that these twenty-six headings are not a revision of the twenty-four propositions discussed so thoroughly over the previous year, nor even derived from them. Nor were the twenty-six paragraphs and the headings listed above simply created from nothing at this brief meeting in Zurich. Instead they derived directly from a set of twenty paragraphs or articles which Calvin had sent to a meeting in Bern in March of 1549, with an exceedingly diplomatic cover letter.[2] This introduces a major new component into these bilateral discussions. Why the sudden shift from the twenty-four propositions they had been debating to the twenty paragraphs from the Bern synod? Calvin's letter of 7 May suggesting his trip to Zurich made no mention of the Bern articles; on the contrary, it implied that he and Bullinger were about to conclude a verbal agreement on their own twenty-four propositions. Perhaps the impasse discussed above proved intractable after all, whether to Calvin or to Bullinger. Yet the resolution in Zurich was too brief to permit both a stalemate over one text and then also a new start on a fresh text. Perhaps before the meeting even began, the principals had decided to work from the Bern articles, although this is pure conjecture.

More concretely, perhaps the time had simply and urgently come for a wider alliance, for multilateral talks instead of bilaterals. Calvin and Bullinger were only two, albeit major, negotiators in the much larger and more complicated context of Swiss Reformed relationships. Besides Geneva and Zurich, Bern was one of several other important ecclesiastical centres in Swiss Protestantism, and thus in the defence against the emperor's armies and his Roman Catholic compromises. In fact, the complex relationship between Calvin and the Bern clergy and senate is particularly pertinent to this entire discussion. As close neighbors, Geneva and Bern found their every doctrinal dispute to be exacerbated by jurisdictional implications. Staunchly Zwinglian from the start, the Bern leaders had quelled a movement sympathetic to Luther, and were vigilant ever after regarding such leanings. Some of the clergy and especially some members of the senate,

---

[1] The Latin text is in CR 35: 733-748, and in Calvin's *Opera Selecta*, ed. P. Barth and W. Niesel (Munich: C. Kaiser, 1952) II: 241-258. It will be cited by paragraph number without further reference to those columns. English translations of the *Consensus Tigurinus* are provided in Calvin's *Tracts and Treatises* Vol. II, ed. by H. Beveridge (repr. Grand Rapids: Eerdmans, 1958), 212-220; and in the *Journal of Presbyterian History* 44 (1966): 45-61, by Ian Bunting, who included this translation in his (unpublished) Th.M. thesis at Princeton Theological Seminary in 1960.

[2] The text of the Bern articles is in CR 35: 717-722 and will be cited by paragraph number without further references to those columns. Calvin's cover letter of 13 March 1549 is in CR 41: 216-218; Bonnet II, 214f.

which ratified any alliance, were suspicious of Calvin as too Lutheran regarding the Supper. He was thought a crypto-Philippist, so to speak. Thus Calvin's overture to the Bern synod, to which he was pointedly not invited, concerned the same topic and many of the same dynamics as his initiatives with Bullinger. Pushing this argument even further, Ulrich Gabler theorizes that Calvin saw the opportunity to strike an agreement with the moderate Zwinglians in Zurich as leverage with the extreme Zwinglians in Bern and with his own opponents in Geneva, since they would surely need to go along with Zwingli's home city.[1]

Yet here too caution is required. Even though these articles were originally prepared for the Bern meeting and were sent to Haller as the head pastor, they were never presented there, much less accepted as part of some other alliance taking shape before the Geneva-Zurich meeting. Haller wrote both Bullinger and Calvin that he had decided against presenting Calvin's articles, for fear of further controversies.[2] Still, the need for multilateral agreement was plain, as seen by the acceptance of this *Consensus* by other cities, even eventually Bern, after Calvin's sudden trip to Zurich in May of 1549.

The text of this agreement has received numerous interpretations, some of them quite unrelated to its context. A thorough exegesis of the *Consensus Tigurinus* must include two specific questions: First, how does this document differ textually from its parent text, Calvin's Bern articles? Second, how does it compare conceptually with the positions taken by Bullinger and Calvin during their previous correspondence and negotiations discussed at length above? Of course, these two questions may be intertwined if, for example, Bullinger introduced some change into Calvin's Bern articles in order to maintain his prior positions.

In a collation of the twenty-six articles of this joint statement with the twenty of Calvin's unsuccessful proposal to Bern, the first six articles of the Zurich consensus show no direct literary relationship with any prior text. They seem to have arisen directly from the Zurich meeting. Conceptually, they expand in detail upon the Christological emphasis in Calvin's second article to Bern, but without its reference to Christ's 'substance', which Bullinger much later remembered as objectionably 'Bucerian.'[3] Article 5, on Christ communicating himself to us, was proposed by Calvin after the actual May meeting, and was accepted by the Zurich leadership, as discussed below. Although this article states clearly that 'we are made one with him, and are engrafted into his body,' it does so as part of the Christological introduction, before the sacraments themselves are introduced, thus apparently honouring Bullinger's aversion to binding this spiritual process of grace too closely to the external sacraments.

Article 6 makes the transition from communion with Christ to the sacraments by saying that preaching was instituted and the sacraments commended to us 'for the sake of testifying to this' communion. An opening presentation of the sacraments in terms of testifying was obviously Bullinger's preference. To preview the rest, articles 7-9 have a complicated relationship of derivation and

---

[1] 'Das Zustandekommen,' 323f., and TRE 8: 189 (see note 1 on p.5 above).
[2] Haller to Bullinger, 7 March 1549, CR 41: 214; Haller to Calvin, 29 April 1549, CR 41: 242f.
[3] Bouvier, 562.

opposition with Calvin's Bern articles 1, 3, and 5, respectively. Zurich articles 10-21 and 24-26 derive directly from the previous texts nos. 6-20, with only brief editorial changes, whether stylistic and irrelevant or else substantive and revealing.

Article 7 begins with two Zwinglian themes, that the sacraments are 'marks and witnesses' of the Christian community, and that they recall Christ's death to our memory, so that faith might be exercised. Such a Zwinglian starting point is curious. Neither of these themes received much attention in Bullinger's own work, except when he had been defending Zwingli. Perhaps this was another occasion to honour his predecessor's legacy, at least in passing. Bullinger's personal loyalties may have been renewed that very spring, when his daughter married the younger Ulrich Zwingli[1]. Yet Calvin's own observation on the internal dynamics of the Zurich delegation suggests another explanation for these traces of Zwinglianism: 'had the rest imitated the calmness of Bullinger, I should have obtained all more easily.'[2] The title of the *Consensus* clearly indicates that this was not a bilateral agreement between Calvin and Bullinger alone, but rather between Calvin and the ministers of the church at Zurich. Were some of these others more Zwinglian than Bullinger was, and indeed more Zwinglian than Bullingerian?

In any case, the heart of article 7 goes beyond these Zwinglian expressions to say that the principal end of the sacraments is to 'testify, represent, and seal' God's grace to us. This continuation of the theme of testimony was already in Calvin's Bern articles, but was amplified here by the addition of 'represent' and by the characterization of the sacraments as 'living images before our eyes,' almost as visual aids to confirm and ratify the announcement of the Word. This too is clearly consistent with Bullinger's overall emphasis. Calvin had depicted the sacraments as testimonies in the document sent to the Bernese because they were harboring the same objections to Calvin's instrumentalism as Bullinger was. As discussed earlier, the Bern articles were already Calvin's attempt at compromise on these same points. He had tried to blend the emphases on testimony and on instrument, but since the latter met with Haller's direct objection, the Bern initiative failed.[3] Although not successful at Bern, this compromise text apparently commended itself to the Zurich theologians as the starting point for their session with Calvin. Nevertheless, they were still sensitive to any lingering form of instrumentalism in this 'draft' text, for they edited the Bern articles carefully, as seen in this seventh article and throughout. Thus a compromise document was here subjected to further negotiations.

Article 8, for example, was partly a direct quotation from Calvin's Bern article 3 on partaking of Christ as the font of all blessings, etc., but was also a rewriting of Calvin's first article in that earlier text. There, in Calvin's original wording, the

---

[1] The wedding was on 7 June 1549; Diary, 37. See note 1 on p.17 above, for the traditional account that Bullinger took Zwingli's widow and two children into his own home.
[2] Calvin to Bucer, CR 41, 439, Bonnet II, 235.
[3] Haller's rejoinder to Calvin's articles, CR 41, 722.

sacramental testimonies and seals are true because 'that which they figure is truly offered to us'. This, a favoured expression of Calvin's, was not accepted into the eighth Zurich article, where these testimonies are considered true because the Lord 'performs internally by his Spirit what the sacraments figure to the eyes and other senses.' Article 16 also replaced Calvin's earlier (Bern) phrase 'the sacraments to them [the elect] alone present what they offer' with the less instrumental phrase 'the elect perceive what the sacraments offer.' For Calvin, as already apparent, 'exhibit' involved a closer tie between the sacraments and grace than Bullinger ever conceded. For Calvin 'to exhibit' meant 'to present' or 'to set forth.'[1] The wording they agreed on ('the Lord performs internally by his Spirit') may have left the early Zwingli far behind, but it permitted Bullinger's understanding of the sacrament as an external perceptible analogy to the internal invisible work of the Spirit.

Similarly, article 9 changed Calvin's Bern article 5 quite substantially, first by omitting his insistence that what is signified and promised is in fact fulfilled and presented in the sacrament, and secondly by altering the remaining text. Calvin had originally written, 'Whoever rightly and faithfully uses the sacraments receives Christ, since he is offered there to us, along with his spiritual gifts.' The wording which came out of the Zurich meeting reads, 'all who in faith embrace the promises offered there receive Christ spiritually, with his spiritual gifts.' Here was the Calvin-Bullinger difference at its briefest: not that the sacrament is a means of receiving Christ, but that faith in the promise there offered and illustrated is a means of receiving Christ spiritually. Article 10 continues the discussion of Calvin's Bern item 6 on the importance of the promise over against the 'bare signs,' but omits the latter text's clear use of *per sacramenta* in its opening clause: 'through the sacraments we become participants in Christ and his spiritual gifts.' Months before, Bullinger had explicitly and sharply objected to the preposition 'through' in this sense of a sacramental instrumentality for participating in Christ. He did not relent here, and the entire clause was omitted.

Article 11 ('One should not be awed at the elements') is unchanged from Calvin's Bern no. 7, except that the 'papists' are no longer identified explicitly, probably allowing Zurich suspicions of the Lutherans or even Bucer to be included by implication. In articles 12-14, the text pursues the dialectic represented in the title given to article 13: 'God uses the implement, but such that all the virtue is God's'. Here Calvin's lifelong concern for the sacraments as *instrumenta* and his explicit use of that term in his Bern article 9 was offset by his original dialectic in the Bern text that, nevertheless, 'the entire work of our salvation ought to be considered ascribed to [God] alone (article 13), and by the Zurich substitution of the term *organa* (implement) for instrument.

This substitution bears examination. Bullinger had often objected to both 'instrument' and 'implement.' The former term had been the focus of more disagreement, but the latter was treated as a synonym. Yet here the Zurich delegation agreed to or even insisted upon the substitution of 'implement' for 'instrument'. For some reason, they could accept the former, but not the latter. Either these words were rough synonyms, and Bullinger here yielded to Calvin's instrumental view of the sacraments while yet avoiding the word 'instrument,' or else some shade of meaning was different enough to permit Bullinger to use the word 'implement' without adopting 'instrumentalism.' Short of finding an explicit discussion of these two terms by Calvin and/or Bullinger, our view of this substitution must depend upon the document as a whole. Article 14 illustrates the dialectic of these three articles (12-14) and indeed the balancing act of the entire document.

> We determine therefore that it is Christ alone who truly baptizes internally, who makes us participants of himself in the Supper, who therefore fulfills what the sacraments figure; he uses these aids such that the entire effect resides in his Spirit.

Here too Bullinger finally accepted what had been objectionable terminology, namely, the designation of the sacraments as 'aids' (*adminicula*, here and in article 12), but only when it was also said that 'the entire faculty for acting remains with [God] alone' (article 12).

Article 14 also repeats the characterization of an internal (*intus*) baptism, and then goes on to an apparently instrumentalist view of the Supper: Christ 'makes us participants of himself in the Supper' (*in coena*, which Calvin later identified as Augustinian language [CR 37: 23]. This expression is repeated in article 19: 'Christ communicates himself to us in the Supper.' Although the principal point of the latter article is that Christ also does this before and apart from the Supper, it could be that in these two cases, Bullinger accepted Calvin's fuller view of the sacrament as the very means, or at least a means, of communicating in Christ. Yet Bullinger's subsequent writings, and other points within the text, do not suggest that he was finally convinced by Calvin on this crucial point. Like his agreement to the words 'implement' and 'aid,' perhaps this was Bullinger's effort at compromise, here in two secondary articles, for the sake of an agreement. It is also possible, however, that Bullinger understood *in coena* not to mean 'in the supper' in any (Calvinist) sense of instrumentalism, as in 'by means of the supper,' but to mean simply 'during the supper.' Such, at least, was the meaning of the preposition 'in' somewhat later in the phrase *in actu ipso*, 'during the act itself' (article 20). The flexibility of this language would permit Calvin's viewpoint, but would also permit Bullinger's view of the sacraments not as instruments but as testimonies by analogy, although here the testimony seems to be a simultaneous one, which met his objection before regarding the word *simul*.[1] Yet even here the larger point of article 20 is Bullinger's opposition to a strictly simultaneous relationship between the administration of the sacraments and the action of grace.

Articles 15 and 16 continue this pattern. From Bullinger's point of view, when Calvin's Bern article 11 became Zurich article 15 it was strengthened by adding that nothing of our salvation is transferred from its author to creatures *or elements*. In article 16, reference to what the sacraments 'exhibit' or 'offer' was changed, as examined above regarding article 8. The title of article 17, 'The sacraments do not confer grace,' suggests, incorrectly, a clear victory for Bullinger,

---

[1] See Tylenda's discussion of *exhibeo* in Calvin on page 31 of his article documented in note 2 on p.5 above and previously mentioned in note 3 on p.25 above.

[2] Proposition no. 9 of the twenty-four discussed by Calvin and Bullinger in 1548; see notes 5 on p.35 and 1 and 2 on p.36 above.

who had urged this negation all along against Calvin's consistent arguments for the sacraments as God's way of conferring grace. The title is misleading because the body of the text, taken over completely from Calvin's Bern no. 13, says only that the sacraments do not confer grace upon *all*, which would include the reprobate, as also discussed in the next article (no. 18). The articles had no titles whatsoever in the earlier edition for the Bern synod, but were given their current titles, misleadingly in this case, only for the Zurich consensus. That the sacraments do not confer grace on all was no defeat for Calvin. On whether the sacraments confer grace on the elect or not, the text is shrewdly silent. That explicit issue would have required a dramatic concession by Calvin or Bullinger.

Articles 19 and 20 have already been discussed. Article 21 rejects a local presence, consistent with both Calvin and Bullinger. Article 22 interprets the words of institution figuratively, by 'metonymy.' Like article 5, article 23 was Calvin's proposal after the Zurich meeting was over. The title, 'On the Eating of Christ's Flesh,' might suggest that Calvin was making a final, indeed late, attempt to express his stronger understanding of the sacraments as the actual means of communing in Christ's body. He proposed this article, he wrote Bullinger later that summer, because 'so far there has been no mention of the reality/thing itself, since it has been called a sign, and especially since there has been no word in the entire document about the eating of the flesh.'[1] As such, it could have met with objections from Bullinger. Instead, the text of Calvin's proposed addition was approved by Bullinger, surely because it refers to eating and drinking of Christ's flesh and blood with the crucial qualifier, 'which are here figured.' Thus the eating and drinking of bread and wine remain a figure or analogy for eating and drinking Christ's body and blood, not the means or instrument for it.

Article 24, taken over whole from Calvin's Bern no. 18, opposed transubstantiation and other (Lutheran) follies such as locating Christ under bread or coupling him with bread. Here Calvin seeks to persuade Bern and Zurich how little he has in common with the Lutherans. Article 25 was taken over from its predecessor text (no. 19) with a slight editorial change. Calvin had always been careful not to express his understanding of heaven in simplistic spatial terms. The ascension of Christ's body to heaven did imply distance, but Calvin never put it as baldly as in the Zurichers' addition of a phrase, 'is contained in heaven as in a place.' The final article (no. 26) expressed the common Reformation aversion to adoring the bread, and the common Reformed suspicions of the Lutherans on this point, but does so in terms more frequent in Zurich than in Calvin's writings, 'the bread is placed before us as a symbol and pledge.'

## AFTERMATH AND CONCLUSION
In this light, the *Consensus Tigurinus* can hardly be called Calvin's clear victory in the sixteenth-century Reformed debate over the Lord's Supper, whether over

---

[1] 6 July 1549, CR 41: 306.

Zwingli's lingering influence or over Bullinger's own substantial position.[1] Certain of its articles do represent a finely balanced dialectic between Calvin's concern for the sacraments as God's means or instruments for conferring grace (on the elect), and Bullinger's concern to counteract any transfer of God's saving activity to the creaturely realm. Witness, for example, the alternating emphases in article 12:

'Furthermore, if something of good is conferred upon us through the sacraments, this does not occur because of their own proper virtue, even if you comprehend the promise by which they are characterized. It is God alone who acts by his Spirit, and although he uses the ministry of the sacraments, in this he neither infuses his own power into them, nor detracts anything from the efficacy of his Spirit; but because of our ignorance he adds them as aids, but such that the entire faculty of acting remains with himself alone.'

Yet even here, in this balancing act of Calvin's concerns with Bullinger's, the real resolution of their long-standing differences regarding the sacraments seems to have resulted from Calvin's willingness to omit certain phrases previously essential in his formulations, and yet always objectionable to Bullinger. Completely missing from the *Consensus* were Calvin's usual references to the actual presenting ('exhibiting') of what is signified, to the sacraments as 'instruments' although they are called 'implements', and as that through which God acts in conferring grace. By itself, the absence of a particular word or phrase may not mean a doctrinal compromise but rather a successful negotiation for the contents of one's position with new terminology. Certainly Calvin's work on the *Zurich Consensus* has often been seen this way. Yet the absence of several of Calvin's key expressions may also indicate the extent of Bullinger's success, although the achievement of any agreement at all should certainly be credited more to Calvin than to Bullinger. A modern assessment of who 'won' and who 'lost' is always risky. On that point, the participants' own comments are instructive. Such comments are numerous in this case, for considerable reflection and even further negotiations followed the May meeting, as Calvin and Bullinger gradually revised, edited, published, defended, and interpreted their agreed text.

There are several indications that Calvin himself viewed the May colloquy in Zurich as a compromise by omission on his part, namely, his proposed additions of a foreword, an afterword, and the two paragraphs discussed above (nos. 5 and 23), as well as his private correspondence with Bucer and others. On the way home from Zurich, Calvin shared the text with Viret in Lausanne, who rejoiced but also pointed out what might profitably be added. By invoking this third

---

[1] Calvin is presented as the winner in Kolfhaus, 'Der Verkehr Calvins mit Bullinger,' p.69 (note 3 on p.18 above). Bouvier sees it as mutual, but without a penetrating theological analysis. Niesel says that Calvin's full doctrine was not in the *Consensus Tigurinus: Calvins Lehre vom Abendmahl*, 2nd ed., (Munich: C. Kaiser, 1935), 54f., n. l. See Grass, p.211. For an example of the older view, and survey of prior literature, see Alexander Barclay, *The Protestant Doctrine of the Lord's Supper* (Glasgow: Jackson, Wylie and Co., 1927), chapter 12, 158-179.

party, Calvin diplomatically proposed to Bullinger the addition of an article on 'How Christ communicates himself to us,' which became no. 5 and an article 'On the eating of Christ's flesh, which became no. 23, both discussed in context above. In this letter of 6 July 1549, Calvin also submitted several smaller changes for Bullinger's approval, and urged publication in this augmented form.

Meanwhile, the ministers in Zurich had their own changes to recommend. Their letter to Calvin of 7 July told of the initial reaction of another third party, the Bern clergy. Haller and especially Musculus approved of the contents of the agreement, although not with the foreword by Calvin. Yet the Bernese disapproved of publication, since it would stir up a new commotion, especially with their city magistrates who still suspected Calvin and Farel of Lutheran sympathies.[1] Haller also wrote directly to Calvin, diplomatically explaining that because the magistrates' approval was required, some clergy would not sign, even though they did not disapprove of the contents. Thus he, who approved, could not sign for fear of schism.[2]

The Zurichers, however, wrote Calvin that perhaps a different foreword and afterword would secure the Bern consent. This would seem to have been unrealistic, given the Bern rejection of Calvin's twenty articles so recently. But Zurich's own interests in persuading Calvin to drop his preface are also apparent. Calvin's original preface, perhaps composed on the spot in Zurich, had immediately claimed that the joint statement on the sacraments 'does not contain everything which could usefully and aptly be said, and which otherwise perfectly fits their true understanding.'[3] To suppress this disclaimer, to begin with a different tone, and to satisfy the Bern objections, the Zurich clergy suggested a letter from Calvin to themselves as the new preface or introduction, and one in response from them to him as the new afterword or conclusion. Indeed, they outlined the contents of these letters in some detail.[4] Calvin should write that since to certain people his doctrine of the sacraments seemed to disagree with that of the Zurich clergy and with other ministers in Switzerland, he and Farel approached Zurich and conferred with them on points of reputed or past differences; further, that they all discovered their harmony in the Lord, as Calvin has written up in a brief statement which he (in this letter/preface) recommends sharing with other churches, unless his Zurich colleagues disagree. As for their proposed letter to replace Calvin's afterword as the new conclusion, the Zurichers would acknowledge Calvin's transcription as accurately expressing their agreement, and, while not opposing publication, would circulate it directly

---

[1] There were seven letters from Bern to Zurich in June of 1549, whether from the clergy generally, Haller alone or Musculus alone, whether to the Zurichers generally or to Bullinger alone: CR 41: 287-291, 303f., 312-316. See also 329-331, and a September letter, 391f.

[2] Haller to Calvin, 14 July 1549, CR 41: 326-328. Bonnet (II, 239) mistranslates CR 41: 333 so that Haller is concerned not for schism, but for someone named Schirma.

[3] Original preface, CR 35, XLIX-L. Yet Gäbler considers this first preface and postface never published, 'Das Zustandekommen,' n. 51.

[4] CR 41: 320-322.

to various colleagues in Swiss churches in order to demonstrate their consensus and, perhaps, to elicit improvements. These 'letters', they conclude, would satisfy the Bern clergy and thus facilitate wider distribution and assent.

After a month had passed with no word from Calvin, Bullinger wrote of their eagerness for his consent to this plan, and that they were waiting to hear from him before they responded to his proposals of the additional paragraphs (now nos. 5 and 23).[1] In fact, despite his reservations, Calvin had already decided to go along with this proposal, and had written exactly such a letter to the Zurich clergy on 1 August.[2] It then became the introduction to the *Consensus* and has served as such in all its published forms, replacing his original preface. Calvin followed the Zurichers' general suggestions for its contents, but he did not concede that his doctrine seemed to differ from the Zurich clergy *and* with other ministers in Switzerland, which was blatantly part of Bern's agenda. On 13 August, Calvin wrote a private letter to Bullinger about the new preface ('your outline, my colours') and reminded him about the two paragraphs: 'It is especially important, lest some think us shrewdly silent and others rightly desire what is certainly necessary to express.'[3] 'In fact, it was precisely through shrewd silence, at least regarding certain terms, that Calvin gained this overall agreement with Bullinger.

On 30 August, Bullinger and his colleagues drafted their letter which has replaced Calvin's original afterword in all printed editions, following the general outline they had proposed earlier. Further, they mentioned some highlights of the agreement, even making a virtue out of the (newly added) paragraph on the eating of Christ's body.[4] Bullinger too hoped for early publication.[5] After circulating this revised version to the Bernese and others, Bullinger wrote to Calvin on 30 September that they had all approved his new preface and his proposed additions, which seemed to add a 'certain light to the text.'[6] This September letter accompanied a more formal copy of the entire proceedings, including their 30 August letter of conclusion which Bullinger hoped Calvin would ratify. He also reported that the Schaffhausen and St. Gall clergy had approved of everything, with congratulations, but that the Bern ministers still opposed publication. Also citing an anonymous advisor, Bullinger suggested that they postpone publication, but send copies to their French and German colleagues. This, in fact, is how it remained, until 1551. In February and March of that year, Bullinger and Calvin exchanged letters and agreed, without extended discussion, on the publication of their *Consensus*[7]

---

[1] 14 August 1549, CR 41: 349.
[2] Text of Calvin's prefatory letter in CR 35: 734; reservations in letter to Viret, 20 July 1549, Bonnet II, 240f.
[3] '... callide subticuisse ...' CR 41: 348.
[4] The Zurichers' letter as conclusion: CR 35: 745-748.
[5] Bullinger to Utenhove, 31 August 1549, CR 41: 373.
[6] CR 41: 404f.
[7] Bullinger wrote Calvin several times on this subject, principally on 4 and 27 February and 7 March, CR 42: 43f., 55, and 69f. Calvin wrote to Bullinger on 17 February and 4 March, CR 42: 51f. and 74f. See Bonnet II, 305-308.

Meanwhile, Calvin's own thoughts on this entire process were shared in other private correspondence. He had sent a copy of the text and his proposed additions to Bucer, lately in exile in England. Bucer's response in August revealed his mixed judgment; he could see where Calvin had held firm and where he had been loose. While especially commending the two additional paragraphs, Bucer criticized at length the interpretation of heaven as a place, and had another major concern, as well summarized in Calvin's response to Bucer later that fall:

> 'You devoutly and prudently desire that the effect of the sacraments and what the Lord confers to us through (*per*) them be explicated more clearly and more fully than many allow. Indeed it was not my fault that these items were not fuller. Let us therefore bear with a sigh that which cannot be corrected.'[1]

With this comment, Calvin reveals his own reservations about the *Consensus*, even with the two additional articles now in place. He indirectly confirms the above hypothesis that the text significantly omits his concern for the sacraments as the instruments through which God confers the grace of communing with Christ's body. Calvin's comments to Bucer argue against the alternative hypothesis that the substitute of 'implement' for 'instrument' was actually a victory for Calvin's instrumentalism. It seems rather that the absence of terms such as 'instrument,' 'through the sacrament,' and 'presenting/offering' (*exhibeo*) indicates Calvin's concession by omission.

Nevertheless, when the agreement became known, Calvin put the best construction on it and defended it tirelessly. Even before its publication, he defended it against one Susliga and argued that it presented the sacraments as 'instruments,' the very word pointedly *not* in the text.[2] When the agreement was actually published, and the Lutherans attacked it vociferously, Calvin wrote several long treatises, beginning with the 1555 *Defensio* and continuing with essays in 1556, 1557, and 1561. In this first essay he interpreted the *Consensus* from his own 'instrumentalist' point of view, here content to substitute 'implement' for 'instrument,' but repeatedly saying that God confers or works *per sacramenta*, even calling the sacraments the 'means of grace' for being ingrafted into Christ's body,[2] the exact viewpoint omitted in the 1549 agreement with

---

[1] 'Effectum sacramentorum, et quid per ea nobis Dominus conferat, luculentius et uberius explicari quam multi patiantur, pie et prudenter optas. Neque vero per me stetit, quin pleniora quaedam essent. Gemamus ergo ferentes ea quae corrigere non licet.' CR 41: 439. Bucer's letter of 14 August 1549 to Calvin is in CR 41: 350.

[2] Calvin to Susliga, 4 March 1550, CR 41: 535. Yet Calvin here also portrays the agreement in openly Zwinglian-Bullingerian language, suggesting that he had been influenced by these negotiations.

Bullinger.[1] The arguments with the Lutherans Westphal and Heshusius were not over the negative side of Calvin's original dialectic (above, Part I), against a local presence of Christ's body, since Lutheran theology did not really defend a local presence. The dispute was rather over Calvin's proposed resolution of the dialectic, that the believer enjoys a full communion with Christ's absent body through being raised up by the Holy Spirit to heaven.

The Lutherans objected to this *Sursum corda* ascent, as Luther had objected to Oecolampadius at Marburg, not because any Reformed theologian ever suggested that the believers lift up their own hearts in some sort of Pelagian 'self-help.' Such a blatant form of liturgical works-righteousness was never the issue. Rather, the Lutherans argued that communion with Christ is possible only because Christ comes down to communicate himself to us on our level, as Calvin himself summarized later:

'It does not seem to them that Christ is present unless he descends to us. As if, indeed, we do not equally enjoy his presence if he lifts us up to himself.'[2]

Aside from noting that Calvin explicitly rules out self-help, since Christ or Christ's spirit 'lifts us up,' this long and theologically complicated debate between Calvin and the Lutherans cannot be thoroughly explored in this space.

In his public zeal for the agreement, Calvin claimed to the Swiss that Zwingli and Oecolampadius would not have changed a word in it, and insisted to the Lutherans that it would have satisfied Luther's own central concern and even that Luther would have agreed to it.[3] This prompted the Zurichers to wonder if perhaps Calvin was not aware of Luther's full range of comments on the issue,

---

[1] *Defensio sanae et orthodoxae doctrinae de sacramentis*, CR 37: 15-36; English translation by Henry Beveridge, with the *Consensus Tigurinus* (note 1 on p.40 above), 221-244. Specifically, 'gratiae media', CR 37: 20 (Beveridge, 227), 'media vocantur, quibus vel inseramur in corpus Christi', CR 37: 17 (222f.), cf. CR 37: 24 (231); 'organa esse quibus efficaciter agit Deus in suis electis', CR 37: 18 (224); 'per sacramenta nobis confertur', CR 37: 22 (229), 'Deum per sacramenta agere volunt? Hoc docemus', CR 37: 23 (229). See Joseph N. Tylenda, 'The Calvin-Westphal Exchange. The Genesis of Calvin's Treatises against Westphal,' in *Calvin Theological Journal* 9 (1974): 182-209. Tylenda surveys Calvin's correspondence and other sources to reconstruct the chronology and circumstances of this exchange of several treatises during the 1550's. Calvin wrote *Secunda defensio* in 1556 (CR 37: 41-120), *Ultima admonitio* in 1557 (CR 37: 137-252), and *Delucidia explicatio* in 1561 (CR 37: 457-524). Tylenda explicitly identifies this survey as a prolegomenon to an examination to the contents of the works in question. One such examination is in Heinrich Schmid, *Der Kampf der lutherischen Kirche um Luthers Lehre vom Abendmahl in Reformationzeitalter* (Leipzig, 1873)

[2] *Institutes* IV, 17, 31; see also IV, 14, 12, IV, 17, 16 and 18, a letter of 22 August 1553, CR 42: 594, Bonnet II, 419, and the *Geneva Catechism* 53, 355f. (*Opera Selecta*, ed. P. Barth and D. Scheuner, II, 140. For Luther's comment at Marburg, see *Luther's Works* 38: 46.

[3] On Zwingli and Oecolampadius: CR 37: 11f., Bonnet III, 85; on Luther: CR 43: 212f., Bonnet III, 56, and CR 43: 215-217, Bonnet III, 61-63. In this last latter, Calvin chastised Melanchthon for his silence.

since he did not read German, and to send him some choice excerpts in Latin translation. Further, the Zurichers took exception to several specific points in Calvin's defence of their *Consensus* against Westphal, and in response to them Calvin had to modify or defend his wording, such as *realiter*.[1] Their consensus statement in 1549 turned out to be open to several interpretations, even among those who signed it. Despite such ongoing differences within Switzerland, Calvin's lot was now firmly cast with the Swiss, who were gradually overcoming their anti-Bucer, anti-Luther suspicions of Calvin enough to embrace him as one of their own. But the alienation from the Lutherans was now insurmountable, especially since Melanchthon had remained silent, which met with Calvin's direct disdain.

Despite the agreement with Zurich, Calvin had not accomplished his immediate goals of progress with Bern and a general Swiss alliance with France. It did not really advance confessional inclusivity very far, at least not in Calvin's own lifetime.[2] Furthermore, it actually contributed to a confessional exclusivity between the Lutherans and the Reformed. Calvin's earlier dream of a common Reformation doctrine of the Lord's Supper was impossible now. With Bucer in exile and Calvin theologically identified with Reformed Switzerland, the confessional lines were hardening fast within the Reformation, especially the line which divided the Lutherans and the Swiss.

For his part, Bullinger also continued to write about the Lord's Supper after these negotiations with Calvin, although his voluminous output cannot be thoroughly surveyed here. Ironically, in a perfect reversal of their earlier roles, it was Bullinger who attempted to tone down the polemics of Calvin's response to Westphal.[3] In his own writings, Bullinger's section on the Lord's Supper in the *Decades* (V, 9) was written just after the agreement with Calvin, and can profitably be compared with the earlier material (V, 6 and 7) from the 1546 *Absoluta*, as presented above. *Decades* V, 9 ('Of the Lord's Holy Supper') continues Bullinger's consistent emphasis on the Supper as analogy and testimony, and nowhere speaks of the Supper as an instrument, an implement, or means of

---

[1] The Zurichers' critique, and quotations from Luther: CR 43: 272-290; Calvin's response: CR 43, 303-307, Bonnet III, 89-94. Some of Bullinger's editorial suggestions are indicated in the apparatus to the *Defensio* in CR 37: 15-36. This critique did not prevent Bullinger from writing a rather innocuous postscript of support for Calvin's *Defensio* (CR 37: 37-40). See Tylenda on 'The Calvin-Westphal Exchange,' 193.

[2] Against John T. McNeill, who sees Calvin's efforts here as motivated purely by ecumenical goals, and who also disregards any military or political context, *Ecumenical Testimony* (Philadelphia: Westminster, 1974), 17-23.

[3] Bouvier, 151; Tylenda, 'Calvin-Westphal' (see note 3 on p.22 above), 185 and 192ff. Bonnet III, 90. Calvin to the Zurichers, 13 November 1554.

grace.[1] Yet it does not explicitly attack such language. Bullinger wrote Calvin that he omitted certain passages because of Calvin's concerns, and was careful that everything be congruent with their *Consensus*. To emphasize that point, he quoted Calvin during his own conclusion, 'so that everyone might see that we agree.'[2] The quotation from Calvin is rather extraneous to his argument, but it does include the expression 'in this banquet Christ is given unto us to be eaten.'[3] As in the *Consensus* articles 14 and 19 (*in coena*), here the ambiguous preposition 'in' can imply 'by means of' the Supper, as Calvin clearly taught, or simply 'during' the Supper, as Bullinger could apparently concede. The latter meaning would reflect an understanding of the (external) Supper as a simultaneous analogy and testimony to the (internal) working of the Holy Spirit on the recipient.

If such external testimony occurs *simultaneously* with the inner work of the Spirit, this would be a development in Bullinger's thought. Except for this single possibility, the *Decades* document no change or development in Bullinger's sacramental theology during his intense negotiations with Calvin. The usual impression of major change in Bullinger is based on the difference between the 1545 *Wahrhaffte Bekanntnus*, thought to be Bullinger's own unreconstructed Zwinglianism, and the *Decades* V, 6-7 and 9, published in 1551, and thus mistakenly thought to post-date the 1549 *Consensus*. In their true context, the former book's Zwinglianism is not fully indicative of Bullinger's own thought, and the 1546 origins of *Decades* V, 6 and 7 as his *Absoluta* show only the slightest variation from the 1551 *Decades* V, 9, namely a possible simultaneity of the testimony and the grace itself in the latter work.

After letting Calvin take the lead in refuting Westphal, Bullinger also joined the public debate in February of 1556 with his *Apologetica expositio*. Like Calvin's defence, Bullinger's book not only defends the Swiss doctrine of the Lord's Supper, but also criticizes the Lutheran views, especially ubiquity and the communication of attributes. Bullinger's later exchange of several polemical treatises with Johann Brenz on these very points echoed Calvin's debate with Westphal and is also impossible to cover in this space. In contrast to Calvin's *Defensio*, Bullinger's work is more irenic, based extensively upon the witness of the early church fathers, and content to quote the *Consensus* on the sacraments as 'testimonies and seals of grace' (chapter 8) instead of Calvin's 'means of grace' interpretation.[4]

---

[1] *Decades* V, 9, 410, 433, and 467. Bullinger here also continued his explicit identification of heaven as a place, not a state or a condition (448). What was worrisome to the Lutherans and forewarned by Luther (*Short Confession*, LW 38, 306f.) was Bullinger's designation of not only *hoc est* regarding the Lord's Supper, but also 'the Word became flesh' regarding the incarnation, as symbolic language not to be taken as literally true, since God was immutable (436).

[2] 27 February 1551, CR 42: 55.

[3] *Decades* V, 9.476. From Calvin's 1539 *Institutes*.

[4] *Apologetica expositio* (Zurich, 1556), on microfilm at Yale Divinity School, and summarized in Schulze, *Heinrich Bullinger 1504-1575* II, 292-300, who also sketches Bullinger's extended controversy with Brenz.

The *Second Helvetic Confession* is especially indicative of Bullinger's work and influence in this regard. In fact, as a major confession of the Reformed tradition, this document is directly relevant to the much larger question of the influence of the *Consensus Tigurinus* and the relationship of the Calvin-Bullinger negotiations to the Reformed view or views of the Lord's Supper. Originally Bullinger's personal confession of faith in 1561, this statement united all of the Swiss Reformed in 1566, and received wide approval and subscription thereafter under the name *Confessio Helvetica Posterior*. On the one hand, Bullinger may have been influenced by his negotiations with Calvin in some degree. The *Second Helvetic* does say that the faithful recipient not only receives the sign, but also enjoys the thing itself, an assurance dear to Calvin.[1] Yet Bullinger can affirm this, not in Calvin's terms of 'through' or 'instrument' or 'means of grace,' terms which do not occur in this sense in the entire *Confession*, but rather in his own terms of an analogy or testimony. In the sacraments, God 'outwardly represents, and, as it were offers unto our sight those things which inwardly he performs unto us.[2] This parallelism of internal and external runs throughout the document as indeed the basis of its sacramental theology.

'And this is outwardly [*foris*] represented unto us by the minister in the sacrament, after a visible manner, and, as it were, laid before our eyes to be seen, which is inwardly [*intus*] in the soul invisibly performed by the Holy Spirit. Outwardly [*foris*] bread is offered by the minister. . . . And meanwhile inwardly [*intus interim*] by the working of Christ through the Holy Spirit, they receive also the flesh and blood of the Lord, and do feed on them unto eternal life.'[3]

The bread is outwardly offered and testifies to an inner nourishment; meanwhile [*interim*] this inward spiritual nourishment is actually taking place. Bullinger echoed Calvin's *sursum corda* theme here,[4] but always stopped short of Calvin's insistence that the external eating is the means or instrument by which God accomplishes the inward feeding. He does, however, seem to affirm a close temporal relationship. Did Bullinger use 'meanwhile' (*interim*) as a synonym for 'at the same time' (*simul*)? If so, the evolution of Bullinger's thought, and perhaps therefore the influence of Calvin and the *Consensus Tigurinus*, consists in this,

---

[1] The *Second Helvetic Confession* in *Bekenntnisschriften und Kirchenordnungen* ed. W. Niesel, 2ed. (Zurich: Zollikon, 1938), ch. 21, p. 265, line 24-26.

[2] *Second Helvetic*, ch. 19, p. 259, line 5f.

[3] *Second Helvetic*, ch. 21, p. 263, line 46 to p. 264, line 12. Ernst Koch comments on this very point: 'Die Sakramentslehre der Confessio als Ganzes basiert auf dem dualismus von intus und foris. Dieses Gegensatzpaar bzw. das damit identische von exterius und interius zieht sich wie ein roter Faden durch all Ausfuehrungen hindurch.' *Die Theologie der Confessio Helvetica Posterior* (Neukirchen-Vluyn: Neukirchener Verlag, 1968), p. 318. See Koch's mention of parallelism on 277-280, the reference to a Schauspiel on 296, and the entire discussion on 293-329.

[4] For the influential after-life of this *sursum corda* motif in the Reformed doctrine of the Lord's Supper, especially Calvin, Cranmer, and Jewel, see Gordon E. Pruett, 'Protestant Doctrine of the Eucharistic Presence,' in *Calvin Theological Journal* 10 (1975): 167-174.

that here the parallelism or analogy is simultaneous. Bullinger had earlier objected to the term *simul* in Calvin's 1548 propositions, as he read it.[1] Yet later, here in the *Second Helvetic Confession,* Bullinger not only tolerates but proposes a sort of simultaneity of sacramental sign and spiritual reality. If, however, *interim* does not imply simultaneity or as close a temporal relationship as *simul,* then Bullinger's position evolved very little throughout his entire life, through a close relationship to Zwingli's legacy and close negotiations with Calvin.

Bullinger's persistent dialectic of the inner and invisible as related to the outer and visible has prompted Brian Gerrish to identify a third type of Reformed view of the Lord's Supper, besides Zwingli's memorialism and Calvin's instrumentalism, namely Bullinger's parallelism.[2] Zwingli had also spoken of the external and the internal, but always as antagonists, whereas Bullinger considered them to be analogous and complementary partners in the sacrament, and Calvin held the one to be the very instrument for the other.

The basic difference in sacramental theology between Calvin and Bullinger endured beyond these negotiations and their agreement on a text. Although alternative interpretations are possible, the most coherent assessment of the overall process is that they achieved a consensus statement principally because Calvin agreed to omit a crucial component of his position. Nevertheless, it was a major accomplishment, and one of historical significance. Calvin was both a prophet and a propagandist when he wrote to Bullinger, 'at least posterity will have a testimony of our faith which did not come from contentious disputations.'[3] As for posterity, the *Second Helvetic Confession* and other Reformed confessions, such as the four written between 1559 and 1563, as well as more modern statements of sacramental theology, should be examined in light of the original consensus and its background in the negotiations between Calvin and Bullinger. The existence of a consensus statement does not necessarily unite the principals and their successors in a single doctrine; basic distinctions may persist below the surface. Does a given Reformed statement of faith consider the Lord's Supper as a testimony, an analogy, a parallel, even a simultaneous parallel to the internal workings of God's grace in granting communion with Christ? If so, the actual ancestor may be Heinrich Bullinger, Zwingli's successor in Zurich. Or does it explicitly identify the Supper as the very instrument or means through which

---

[1] Proposition 9, see notes 4 and 5 on p.35 and 1 on p.36 above. A further, explicit statement of parallelism is in Bullinger's *Summa,* Pestalozzi, 520.

[2] Gerrish, 'Sign and Reality: The Lord's Supper in the Reformed Confessions', in *The Old Protestantism and the New,* see note 2 on p.5 above. On the one hand, Gerrish characterizes this difference as similar to the differences between the Schoolmen, with the Thomist Reformed advocating instrumentalism and the Franciscan Reformed advocating parallelism. On the other hand, Gerrish means to draw a major conceptual line not between Luther and Calvin, who both taught instrumentalism, but between Calvin and Bullinger.

[3] CR 41: 307. Calvin and Bullinger had their share of contentious disputations, on this and other points of doctrine. See G. Locher, 'Bullinger and Calvin,' *Heinrich Bullinger 1504-1575* II, 1-33, and Cornelius Venema, 'Heinrich Bullinger's Correspondence on Calvin's Doctrine of Predestination, 1551-1553,' *The Sixteenth Century Journal* 17 (1986): 435ff.

God offers and confers the grace of full communion with Christ's body? The lineage would then go back to John Calvin, despite the opposition he faced among his Reformed brethren on this very point. Of course, it would take another study entirely to investigate the Reformed tradition in this light, not to mention the complex debates of Calvin and Westphal, of Bullinger and Brenz, and of subsequent Reformed and Lutheran theologians through the centuries. Even such a daunting list of desirable historical studies is still preliminary to the intricate questions of Lutheran and Reformed relationships in the present and the future.

# Appendix: Bibliography of Secondary Sources

Wayne Baker, *Bullinger and the Covenant* (Ohio State University Press, Ohio, 1981).

Alexander Barclay, *The Protestant Doctrine of the Lord's Supper* (Jackson, Wylie and Co., Glasgow, 1927).

Hans Georg vom Berg, 'Spätmittelalterliche Einflüsse auf die Abendmahlalehre des jungen Bullinger in *Kerygma und Dogma* 22 (1976); 221-233.

Ernst Bizer, *Studien zur Geschichte des Abendmahlstreits im 16, Jahrhundert* (2nd ed., Wissenschaftliche Buchgesellschaft, Darmstadt, 1962).

Fritz Blanke, *Der junge Bullinger* (Zwingli Verlag, Zurich, 1942).

Andre Bouvier, *Henri Bullinger le successeur de Zwingli* (E. Droz, Paris, 1940).

Mark S. Burrows, ' "Christus intra nos. vivens". The Peculiar Genius of Bullinger's Doctrine of Sanctifiction.' *Zeitscrift für Kirchengeschichte* 98 (1987): 48-69.

Fritz Büsser, 'Bullinger, Heinrich (1504-1575)' in *Theologische Realenzyklopädie* 7 (1981): 375-387.

Carlos Eire, *War against Idols; The Reformation of Worship from Erasmus to Calvin* (Cambridge University Press, Cambridge, 1986).

Ulrich Gäbler, 'Der junge Bullinger und Luther' in *Lutherjahrbuch* (1975): 131-140.

—, 'Das Zustandekommen des Consensus Tigurinus im Jahre 1549' in *Theologische Literaturzeitung* 104, no. 5 (1979): 321-332.

—, 'Consensus Tigurinus' in *Theologische Realenzyklopädie* 8 (1981): 189-192.

Translated by Ruth C. L. Gritsch, *Huldrych Zwingli, His Life and Work*, (Fortress Press, Philadelphia, 1986).

Ulrich Gäbler, and Erland Herkenrath, *Heinrich Bullinger, 1504-1575, Gesammelte Aufsätze zum 400, Todestaq* (2 vols., Theologischer Verlag, Zurich, 1975).

Brian A. Gerrish, 'Gospel and Eucharist: John Calvin on the Lord's Supper' in *The Old Protestantism and the New: Essays on the Reformation Heritage* (University of Chicago Press, Chicago, 1982).

—, 'The Pathfinder: Calvin's Image of Martin Luther' in *The Old Protestantism and the New; Essays on the Reformation Heritage* (University of Chicago Press, Chicago, 1982).

—, 'Sign and Reality: The Lord's Supper in the Reformed Confessions' in *The Old Protestantism and the New; Essays on the Reformation Heritage* (University of Chicago Press, Chicago, 1982).

—, 'John Calvin and the Reformed Doctrine of the Lord's Supper', in *Una Sancta* 25, no. 2 (1968): 27-39.

Hans Grass, *Die Abendmahlslehre bei Luther und Calvin* (2nd edition, C. Bertelsmann, Gütersloh, C. Bertelsmann, 1954).

Ernst Koch, *Die Theologie der Confessio Helvetica Posterior*, (Neukirchener Verlag, Neukirchen-Vluyn, 1968).

Wilhelm Kolfhaus, 'Der Verkehr Calvins mit Bullinger' in ed. A. Bohatec,*Calvinstudien* (R. Haupt, Leipzig, 1909) 27-125.

Gottfried Locher, *Huldrych Zwingli in Neuer Sicht* (Zwingli Verlag, Zurich, 1968).

—, 'Bullinger und Calvin, Proleme des Vergleichs ihrer Theologien', in *Heinrich Bullinger 1504-1575, Gesammelte Aufsätze zum 400, Todestag,* Vol. 2, *Beziehungen und Wirkungen,* (Zürcher Beitrag zur Reformationsgeschichte, 8, Theologischer Verlag, Zurich, 1975), 1-33.

—, 'Heinrich Bullinger und der Spätzwinglianismus' in *Die Zwinglische Reformation* (Göttingen: Vandenhoeck & Ruprecht, 1979).

—, *Zwingli's Thought, New Perspectives* (Brill, Leiden, 1981).

John T. McNeill, *Ecumenical Testimony* (Westminster, Press, Philadelphia, 1974).

Wilhelm H. Neusner, 'Die Versuche Bullingers, Calvins und der Strassburger, Melanchthon zum Fortgang von Wittenberg zu Bewegen' in *Heinrich Bullinger 1504-1575, Gesammelte Aufsätze zum 400, Todestaq,* Vol. 2, *Beziehungen und Wirkungen* (Zürcher Beitrag zur Reformationsgeschichte, 8 Theologischer Verlag, 1975), 35-55.

Haiko A. Oberman, 'The "Extra" Dimension in the Theology of Calvin' in *Journal of Ecclesiastical History* 21 (1970): 43-64.

Hughes Oliphant Old, 'Bullinger and the Scholastic Works on Baptism: A Study in the History of Christian Worship' in *Heinrich Bullinger 1504-1575. Gesammelte Aufsätze zum Todastaq.* Vol. 1, *Leben und Werk* (Zürcher Beitrag zur Reformationsgeschichte, 7. Theologischer Verlag, Zurich, 1975).

Carl Pestalozzi, *Heinrich Bullinger, Leben und ausgewählte Schriften* (Elberfeld, R. L. Fridrichs, 1858).

G. R. Potter, *Huldrych Zwingli* (St. Martin's Press, New York, 1977).

Gordon E. Pruett, 'Protestant Doctrine of the Eucharistic Presence' in *Calvin Theological Journal* 10 (1975): 142-174.

Jill Raitt, 'Three Inter-related Principles in Calvin's Unique Doctrine of Infant Baptism' in *Sixteenth Century Journal* 11 (1980): 51-61.

Heinrich Schmid, *Der Kampf der lutherischen Kirche um Luthers Lehre vom Abendmahl im Reformationszeitalter* (Leipzig, 1873).

Wilhelm A. Schulze, 'Bullingers Stellung zum Luthertum' in *Todestag.* Vol. 2, *Beziehungen und Wirkungen,* (Zürcher Beitrag zur Reformationsgeschichte, 8. Theologischer Verlag, Zurich, 1975), 287-314.

Joachim Staedtke, *Die Theologie des jungen Bullinger* (Zwingli Verlag, Zurich, 1962).

Otto Erich Strasser, 'Der Consensus Tigurinus' in *Zwingliana* 9, no. 1 (1949): 1-16.

Joseph N. Tylenda, 'The Calvin-Westphal Exchange. The Genesis of Calvin's Treatises against Westphal' in *Calvin Theological Journal* 9 (1974): 182-209.

—, 'The Ecumenical Intention of Calvin's Early Eucharistic Teaching.' in (ed. Brian A. Gerrish), *Reformatio Perennis*, (Pickwick Press, Pittsburgh, 1981) 27-47.

Cornelius Venema, 'Heinrich Bullinger's Correspondence on Calvin's Doctrine of Predestination, 1551-1553' in *The Sixteenth Century Journal* 17 (1986): 435-450.

Robert C. Walton, 'Heinrich Bullinger 1504-1575', in (ed. Jill Raitt), *Shapers of Religious Traditions in Germany, Switzerland, and Poland 1560-1600* (Yale University Press, New Haven, 1981).

# Alcuin/GROW Joint Liturgical Studies

All cost £3.25 (US $7) in 1990

## 1987 TITLES

1. **(LS 49) Daily and Weekly Worship—from Jewish to Christian**
   by Roger Beckwith, Warden of Latimer House, Oxford

2. **(LS 50) The Canons of Hippolytus**
   edited by Paul Bradshaw, Professor of Liturgics, University of Notre Dame

3. **(LS 51) Modern Anglican Ordination Rites**
   edited by Colin Buchanan, then Bishop of Aston

4. **(LS 52) Models of Liturgical Theology**
   by James Empereur, of the Jesuit School of Theology, Berkeley

## 1988 TITLES

5. **(LS 53) A Kingdom of Priests: Liturgical Formation of the Laity: The Brixen Essays**
   edited by Thomas Talley, Professor of Liturgics, General Theological Seminary, New York.

6. **(LS 54) The Bishop in Liturgy: an Anglican Study**
   edited by Colin Buchanan, then Bishop of Aston

7. **(LS 55) Inculturation: the Eucharist in Africa**
   by Phillip Tovey, research student, previously tutor in liturgy in Uganda

8. **(LS 56) Essays in Early Eastern Initiation**
   edited by Paul Bradshaw, Professor of Liturgics, University of Notre Dame

## 1989 TITLES

9. **(LS 57) The Liturgy of the Church in Jerusalem**
   by John Baldovin

10. **(LS 58) Adult Initiation**
    edited by Donald Withey

11. **(LS 59) 'The Missing Oblation': The Contents of the Early Antiochene Anaphora**
    by John Fenwick

12. **(LS 60) Calvin and Bullinger on the Lord's Supper**
    by Paul Rorem

## 1990 TITLES

13-14 **(LS 61/62) The Liturgical Portions of The Apostolic Constitutions: A Text for Students**
    edited by W. Jardine Grisbrooke (March 1990)
    This double-size volume provides in effect two of the Studies for 1990, and costs double price (i.e. £6.50 in England in 1990).

15. **(LS 63) Liturgical Inculturation in the Anglican Communion**
    edited by David Holeton, Professor of Liturgics, Trinity College, Toronto (June 1990)
    The Anglican International Liturgical Consultation at York in August 1989 adopted a major statement on liturgical inculturation. 'Down to Earth Worship'. This symposium reprints the Statement and expounds it and applies it to various parts of the Anglican Communion. It is published early, following no. 13-14, in order to be available to the ACC in 1990.

16. **(LS64) Cremation Today and Tomorrow**
    by Douglas Davies, University of Nottingham (December 1990)
    A practical study of attitudes towards cremation, with theological suggestions for new cremation services.

# Grove Liturgical Studies

This series began in March 1975, and was published quarterly until 1986. Nos. 1, 3-6, 10 and 30 are out of print. Asterisked numbers have been reprinted. Prices in 1990, £2.50

## Previous Alcuin titles

## The Alcuin Club

Membership of the Alcuin Club includes the cost of the four Joint Liturgical Studies each year within the annual subscription rate, on a reduced basis, Details from

> The Rev. Tim Barker
> 6 Hillfield
> Norton
> Runcorn
> Cheshire WA7 6RN

(Address after April 1990):

> All Saints Vicarage
> Highlands Avenue
> Runcorn
> Cheshire WA7 4PS